BAKING FOR
Beginners

Publications International, Ltd.

Pictured on the front cover: Double Chocolate Dream Bars *(page 56)*.

Pictured on the back cover *(clockwise from top left):* Refrigerator Cookies *(page 22)*, Classic Yellow Cake *(page 122)*, Chocolate Chip Skillet Cookie *(page 36)*, Ginger Plum Tart *(page 160)*, Glazed Lemon Loaf Cake *(page 134)*, Pumpkin Pecan Crunch Bars *(page 50)*, Brown Butter Blueberry Peach Cobbler *(page 176)*, and Marbled Banana Bread *(page 72)*.

ISBN: 978-1-64558-606-7

Manufactured in China.

8 7 6 5 4 3 2 1

Microwave Cooking: Microwave ovens vary in wattage. Use the cooking times as guidelines and check for doneness before adding more time.

Let's get social!
@Publications_International
@PublicationsInternational
www.pilbooks.com

CONTENTS

BAKING BASICS

Homemade baked goods are one of life's small pleasures. You can always buy sweet treats from the supermarket or a local bakery, but there's something special about having warm cookies fresh from the oven or a birthday cake made from scratch. Baking is a form of tradition, celebration and comfort—and it's fun! You might have heard that baking is an exact science or that baking has more rules than cooking; those things may be true, but they don't mean that baking has to be complicated. You don't need to tackle croissants, rainbow cakes or yeast breads when you're just starting out. Keep it simple! This book is packed with delicious, easy-to-bake recipes that anyone can handle, plus all the basic baking information you'll need for success. From ingredients and equipment to tips and techniques, the following beginner's guide is designed to help get you off to a good start.

ingredients

Keeping your pantry stocked with basic and frequently used ingredients is an important first step in baking.

baking powder

This leavener is made of baking soda and cream of tartar; when combined with liquid ingredients, it releases carbon dioxide gas bubbles that cause baked goods to rise. One teaspoon baking powder per cup of flour is the standard amount required.

baking soda

With four times the leavening power of baking powder, only a small amount of baking soda is needed to make doughs and batters rise. Baking soda is alkaline, so it is used in recipes that contain an acidic ingredient such as buttermilk, sour cream, brown sugar, fruit or chocolate. It is sometimes used in combination with baking powder, but the two are not interchangeable. Both leaveners should be used before the expiration date on the container.

butter

Unsalted butter is preferred so you can control the amount of salt in a recipe. The temperature of the butter is important in baking recipes; whether butter is cold, softened (which is room temperature) or melted greatly affects the texture of your baked goods.

cocoa powder

Natural cocoa powder is more common than Dutch process, which is darker in color, less acidic and preferred by many baking professionals. The two types of cocoa are generally interchangeable in recipes, but there will be some differences in color and flavor—baked goods made with Dutch process cocoa will be darker in color and milder in flavor.

eggs

Eggs are an essential ingredient in baking, contributing structure, richness and moisture to most baked goods. Most recipes assume the use of large eggs, and it's best to have your eggs at room temperature. Baking recipes often have a high fat content, and cold eggs can harden the fat—this may result in curdled batter, which would affect the final texture of your cakes and cookies. Room temperature eggs also whip up to a greater volume than cold eggs when you're beating whole eggs or egg whites for a recipe. To bring eggs to room temperature, you can set them out on the counter for 30 minutes to an hour before baking, or place them in a bowl of warm tap water for 10 to 15 minutes while you're getting your other ingredients ready.

flour

All wheat flours contain the protein gluten, which is important in providing the structure in baked goods. All-purpose flour is the most common; it has a medium gluten content. Cake flour has a low gluten content and is used for more tender cakes and pastries, while bread flour has a high gluten content and is often preferred for breads and pizzas. Whole wheat flour is milled from the entire wheat kernel (bran and germ); it is more perishable than other flours so it should be purchased in small amounts and stored in the refrigerator.

oats

Old-fashioned oats are larger and coarser in texture than quick-cooking oats, which have been rolled into thinner flakes. Both types of oats add texture and flavor to baked goods; recipes will specify which to use (they are frequently interchangeable). Avoid instant and steel-cut oats for baking.

oil

Use neutral-tasting oils such as vegetable, canola or safflower oil in most baking recipes to provide moisture and tenderness without adding additional flavors or aromas. Olive oil is often used in Mediterranean baked goods; it has a distinctive flavor which is an essential part of many breads and cakes from this region.

salt

Salt is a flavor enhancer, so don't be tempted to leave it out. It doesn't make foods taste salty; it wakes up other flavors, creating balance in baked goods while also strengthening gluten, contributing to tenderness and encouraging browning. Unless otherwise specified, use table salt.

sugar

Sugar adds more than sweetness to baked goods; it also adds flavor, moisture and tenderness. Brown sugar is a blend of granulated white sugar and molasses, while powdered sugar (also called confectioners' sugar) is granulated sugar that has been ground to a finer texture and mixed with a small amount of cornstarch to prevent caking. Sparkling sugar is coarse, large-grained white sugar used for topping baked goods to add shine and sweet crunch.

vanilla extract

Pure vanilla extract is made by steeping vanilla beans in alcohol; the resulting extract adds vanilla flavor and enhances other flavors in baked goods. Imitation vanilla is made entirely of artificial flavorings which sometimes have a harsh taste and can leave a bitter aftertaste. Like all extracts, vanilla is very concentrated and should be used in small amounts. Avoid adding vanilla to hot liquids, as some of the vanilla flavor will evaporate along with the alcohol.

equipment

Having the right tools makes baking easier. You don't need a lot of fancy equipment or appliances to be a good baker, but you do need a few essentials—many of which may already be in your kitchen.

baking pans

Square and rectangular metal pans are used for cakes and bar cookies; the most popular sizes are 8 and 9 inches square and 13x9 inches. Square pans are also useful for making half batches of cakes, brownies and bars.

baking sheets

Also known as sheet pans, these metal pans with a low rim (about ½ inch) can be used for everything from cookies and pizza to biscuits and scones. Cookie sheets typically have no rim or a rim on one side. This makes it easy to slide off cookies and biscuits, but the rims on baking sheets mean they can also be used for savory dishes such as roasting vegetables, meat and poultry.

cake pans

Round cake pans that are 8 or 9 inches in diameter and at least 1½ inches high are used for snack cakes and layer cakes. (You'll need at least two pans if you plan on baking layer cakes.) Bundt pans are a type of round tube pan with fluted sides; the standard size is 10 inches in diameter with a 12-cup capacity. The hole in the center helps cakes bake more quickly and evenly. A springform pan is strongly recommended for cheesecakes and other delicate baked goods; it is a round cake pan with an expandable spring-release side that makes it easy to remove cakes from the pan.

loaf pans

Loaf pans are designed for baking quick bread and yeast bread loaves, pound cakes and fruit cakes. A standard loaf pan measures 9x5x3 inches with slightly flared sides; smaller pans measuring 8½x4¼ or 8x4 inches are also common.

measuring cups

You'll need two types of measuring cups for basic baking (and cooking). Dry measuring cups come in nested sets and are used for ingredients such as sugar, flour, oats and peanut butter. Liquid measuring cups are usually made of glass or plastic and are designed for measuring liquids, with measurement markings visible from the outside of the cups.

measuring spoons

Measuring spoons come in nested sets measuring from ¼ teaspoon to 1 tablespoon. Oblong measuring spoons are useful, as they sometimes fit into spice jars when round ones cannot. Don't substitute the teaspoons and tablespoons from your everyday flatware; these spoons don't hold the same amount.

muffin pans

For baking muffins or cupcakes, you'll need a muffin pan, which is a rectangular baking pan with 12 cup-shaped cavities. A standard muffin cup measures 2½ inches in diameter, but giant muffin pans (with 3¼-inch cups) and mini muffin pans (with 1¾-inch cups) are also available.

parchment paper

This heavy paper sold in rolls and sheets is impervious to grease and moisture. When used to line baking sheets and pans, parchment paper provides a nonstick surface, allows for effortless removal of baked goods and makes cleanup much easier.

pastry blender

This hand-held tool consists of several U-shaped wires or metal blades attached to a handle. It is used to cut butter and/or shortening into flour, which is an essential step in making pie dough. Two knives or forks can be used if you don't have a pastry blender.

pie plate

Standard pie plates are 9 inches in diameter and about 1½ inches deep, while deep-dish pie plates are 2 inches deep. Pie plates may be made of glass, ceramic or metal; glass may be the best choice for beginners as it's inexpensive, widely available and produces a crisp, golden brown crust.

rubber or silicone spatula

Spatulas or scrapers are flexible utensils that come in a wide variety of sizes and are useful for blending dough, folding delicate mixtures and cleanly scraping batter out of bowls.

whisk

Whisks are wire tools designed to blend ingredients together—they're good for combining dry ingredients as well as stirring batters or sauces until smooth.

wire cooling rack

A raised metal rack allows air circulation around your baked goods or baking pan, which speeds up cooling and prevents steam accumulation that causes soggy treats.

wooden spoon

The classic tool you use for stirring pasta sauce and taco filling is also great for mixing cookie, brownie and quick bread batters. Make sure you keep a separate one just for baking so you don't get any onion or garlic flavors in your baked goods.

BAKERS' TALK

BEAT Mix ingredients together to blend, smooth and/or soften them, which can be done with a fork, spoon, whisk, spatula or mixer depending on the recipe and the ingredients. Beating uses more speed than simply mixing or combining ingredients and incorporates air into a mixture.

COMBINE Mix ingredients together to blend them.

CUT IN Blend a fat (butter or shortening) into a flour mixture.

CREAM Beat butter or butter and sugar until well blended, aerated and lighter in color (usually done with an electric mixer).

DOT Drop small bits of an ingredient (usually butter) on top of a dish.

DRY INGREDIENTS Ingredients that don't contain liquid (flour, sugar, baking powder, cocoa, etc.).

DUST Sprinkle an ingredient (usually flour or powdered sugar) lightly over a baking pan, work surface or baked good.

FOLD Gently mix ingredients (usually with a rubber spatula) to combine them, avoiding vigorous beating or stirring. Folding is done to incorporate a lighter mixture (such as beaten egg whites or whipped cream) into a heavier mixture (such as cake batter or pie filling).

WET INGREDIENTS Ingredients that contain liquid (oil, eggs, milk, juice, liquid extracts).

getting started

No matter what you choose to bake, there are some important steps you should always take to ensure success:

✔ Always read through the entire recipe before beginning, so you know that you have the necessary ingredients and equipment and you understand the timing involved.

✔ Preheat your oven according to the recipe directions—batters and doughs won't rise, spread or bake properly if the oven isn't hot enough. Using an oven thermometer will help make sure you have the right temperature before baking. Many home ovens are off between 5 and 50 degrees; an oven thermometer allows you to adjust the setting and compensate as necessary.

✔ Check for doneness before the minimum time. Most recipes give a range for baking times, and there are many variables which can affect these numbers—different pan materials, oven fluctuations, the temperature of your ingredients and kitchen, etc. To be safe, check for doneness a few minutes before the recommended time using the test given in the recipe.

cookie smarts

• Unless a recipe directs otherwise, have all ingredients at room temperature (65° to 70°F) so they can combine more easily and produce a smoother dough.

• Avoid overmixing batter or dough, which can result in cookies that are tough or dry or spread too much.

• Create cookies that are uniform in size so they finish baking at the same time.

• For even baking and browning, position an oven rack in the center of the oven and bake only one cookie sheet at a time. If you do use two sheets at a time, rotate them from top to bottom and front to back halfway through the baking time.

• Allow cookie sheets to cool between batches; the dough will spread if it's placed on a hot cookie sheet. (Or buy a few extra cookie sheets so you won't have to wait.)

• For bar cookies, use the pan size called for in the recipe. A smaller pan will result in thick and soggy bars; a larger pan will produce thinner bars with a drier texture. For easier cleanup, line the baking pan with foil or parchment paper.

• Follow recipe directions for removing cookies from cookie sheets. Some thin cutout or refrigerator cookies should be removed from the cookie sheets immediately after baking, but most cookies, particularly larger ones, need to rest on the cookie sheets several minutes to set. Transferring to wire racks is essential; it allows air to flow around the cookies and prevents them from becoming soggy. Bar cookies should cool completely in their pans on wire racks before cutting.

• Cool cookies completely before storing them, and once cool, store soft and crisp cookies separately. Keep soft cookies in shallow airtight containers; store crisp cookies in containers with loose-fitting lids to prevent moisture build-up.

cake savvy

• Position an oven rack just below the center of your oven for even baking. If you're baking two cake layers, make sure there is space between the two pans for heat circulation.

• Have your ingredients at room temperature to ensure a smooth and well blended batter.

• For easy removal, line your round cake pans with parchment paper. Trace the bottoms of the cake pans on parchment paper and cut out the circles. Lightly spray the pans with nonstick cooking spray before placing the parchment rounds inside, then grease and flour the pans (both the parchment and the sides) as the recipe directs. Square and rectangular cakes are often left in the pans for serving, so easy removal is not as important and using cooking spray without parchment paper is sufficient. Bundt, tube and springform pans do not need to be lined with parchment.

• Don't overmix! In general, the butter and sugar in cake recipes need to be well beaten, but the flour and other dry ingredients should be mixed in gently and stirred only until the ingredients are combined. Overmixing will cause the air you've beaten into the batter to deflate and too much gluten to develop, which ultimately leads to tough cakes.

• Smooth out the batter after you've poured or spread it in the pan(s). This will remove any large air cavities, promote even baking and help keep the top of your cake smooth and flat (which looks better and makes it easier to frost).

• Avoid opening the oven door while your cake is baking—this causes drastic temperature fluctuations which disturb the rising process and cause your cake to collapse and sink. Simply follow the recipe and check for doneness at or near the end of the recommended baking time.

• There are several ways to test a cake for doneness. The easiest one is to use a toothpick inserted into or near the center of the cake; it should come out clean or have a few crumbs attached as the recipe directs. Or you can press lightly on top of the cake; if it springs back and doesn't hold the indentation of your fingertips, it's done. A final test is the appearance—a cake is done when it has risen in the center and the edges begin to pull away from sides of pan.

• Cakes should cool in their pans 10 to 15 minutes before inverting them onto a wire cooling rack. If you try to remove a cake from the pan when it's hot, it might split. And if you wait too long, the grease used to coat the pan before baking will harden and can cause the cake to stick.

• Cool cakes completely before frosting, and chill them if you have time. Refrigerating cake layers or freezing them briefly will make them firmer and easier to frost.

• Before frosting or glazing a cake, brush off any excess crumbs from the cake and the plate or platter.

pie & tart pointers

• Keep your dough ingredients cold—that's one of the essential elements that makes a flaky pie crust. The butter and/or shortening should be cold, and you should use ice cold water for the best results. If your kitchen is warm, refrigerating the flour can help too.

• Some pie dough recipes use both shortening and butter. Butter has the best flavor and makes a richer tasting crust, but shortening makes the dough more flaky and easier to work with. A combination of the two can provide the best of both worlds.

• After making the dough, let it rest in the refrigerator before rolling it out. This gives the flour time to absorb all the liquid. After rolling out the crust and lining the pie plate, chill the dough again; this relaxes the dough and helps prevent it from shrinking in the oven.

• A sprinkling of flour is needed on your work surface (and sometimes your rolling pin) in order to roll out the dough without sticking, but use as little as possible so the dough doesn't become tough. Or roll out the dough between two pieces of lightly floured parchment or waxed paper, which helps minimize extra flour usage and makes it easier to move the crust to the pie plate.

• Bake your pies on the lowest oven rack to prevent soggy bottom crusts. Setting the pies on a preheated baking sheet also helps with a well-browned and crisp crust. (And using a baking sheet prevents any filling from leaking on the oven floor.)

• If the edges of your pies are browning too quickly, make a ring out of pieces of aluminum foil to protect the edges while leaving the rest of the pie uncovered.

(If you start to bake pies frequently, you may want to purchase a metal or silicone pie shield to cover the edges instead.)

• Even though warm pies are so tempting, they must cool completely before cutting into them. The fillings need time to set (4 to 6 hours for fruit pies, 2 hours for custard pies), which makes slicing easier (and neater). If you want to serve a pie warm, cover it loosely with foil and heat it in a 300°F oven for 15 minutes before serving.

• Shortcuts are perfectly acceptable! Store-bought refrigerated pie crust is quick and easy; it's a convenience product that works well and tastes good. Some of the pie and tart recipes in the book use made-from-scratch pie dough and some use prepared pie dough. Use what works best for you.

quick bread tips

• Quick breads and muffin batters should be mixed gently and as briefly as possible. They're most commonly made by combining the dry ingredients in one bowl and the wet ingredients in another bowl and mixing them together. This mixture should be stirred only until the dry ingredients are moistened—you don't want to work the gluten too much or deflate the air bubbles that form from the action of the baking powder or baking soda. It's ok if the batter is lumpy. Too much stirring will result in breads with a tough texture and cause muffins to turn out dry with lots of holes and tunnels. Use a rubber spatula or wooden spoon to blend the batter only until no streaks of flour remain.

• The butter and/or shortening in most biscuit and scone recipes must be cold to ensure light and flaky results.

- Biscuit and scone recipe directions call for cutting the fat into a flour mixture, which simply means that the fat is incorporated into the flour mixture without overworking or softening the butter or shortening too much. This can be done with a pastry blender, two knives, a fork or your fingertips; the goal is to end up with small pea-size pieces or coarse crumbs (the recipe will specify the size) before liquid is added. A food processor can also be used to mix a biscuit or scone dough quickly, which helps keep the fat cold and results in lighter biscuits and scones.

- Quick breads (all types) should be baked immediately after mixing. The leaveners (baking powder and/or baking soda) begin to work as soon as the dry and wet ingredients are mixed together, forming carbon dioxide bubbles that make the bread rise. If baking is delayed, the leaveners can lose their power and you may end up with a flatter, denser bread.

- The easiest way to check for doneness in quick breads is with a toothpick; when inserted into the center of a bread or muffin, it should come out clean or with just a few crumbs attached. Raw batter on the toothpick means that the bread needs a little more time. Biscuits and scones are done when their top and bottom crusts are an even golden brown color.

- Most quick bread loaves should be cooled completely (1 to 2 hours) before slicing to prevent crumbling. Smaller breads like muffins, biscuits and scones may be eaten after cooling briefly. For the best results, follow the specific cooling instructions in each recipe.

BAKING SUBSTITUTIONS

IF YOU DON'T HAVE	USE
1 cup cake flour	1 cup minus 2 tablespoons all-purpose flour plus 2 tablespoons cornstarch (Sift before using.)
1 cup packed brown sugar	1 cup granulated sugar mixed with 2 tablespoons molasses
1 cup whole milk	1 cup skim milk plus 2 tablespoons melted butter
1 cup buttermilk	1 cup lemon juice or vinegar plus enough milk to equal 1 cup. (Stir; let stand 5 minutes.)
1 cup sour cream	1 cup plain yogurt
1 ounce unsweetened chocolate	3 tablespoons unsweetened cocoa powder plus 1 tablespoon vegetable oil, butter or shortening
1 ounce semisweet chocolate	1 ounce unsweetened chocolate plus 1 tablespoon sugar

COOKIES

peanutty double chip cookies

makes about 3 dozen cookies

½ cup (1 stick) butter, softened
¾ cup granulated sugar
¾ cup packed brown sugar
2 eggs
1 teaspoon baking soda
1 teaspoon vanilla

2 cups all-purpose flour
1 cup chunky peanut butter
1 cup semisweet or milk chocolate chips
1 cup peanut butter chips

1 Preheat oven to 350°F. Line cookie sheets with parchment paper or spray with nonstick cooking spray.

2 Beat butter, granulated sugar and brown sugar in large bowl with electric mixer at medium speed 2 minutes or until well blended. Add eggs, baking soda and vanilla; beat 2 minutes or until light and fluffy. Add flour and peanut butter; beat at low speed until dough is stiff and smooth. Stir in chocolate and peanut butter chips.

3 Drop dough by heaping tablespoonfuls 2 inches apart onto prepared cookie sheets. Press down with tines of fork to flatten slightly.

4 Bake 12 minutes or until cookies are set but not browned. Remove to wire racks to cool completely.

basic oatmeal cookies

makes 3 dozen cookies

2 cups old-fashioned oats

1⅓ cups all-purpose flour

¾ teaspoon baking soda

½ teaspoon baking powder

½ teaspoon salt

1 cup packed brown sugar

¾ cup (1½ sticks) butter, softened

¼ cup granulated sugar

1 egg

1 tablespoon honey

1 teaspoon vanilla

1 Preheat oven to 350°F. Line cookie sheets with parchment paper.

2 Combine oats, flour, baking soda, baking powder and salt in medium bowl; mix well. Beat brown sugar, butter and granulated sugar in large bowl with electric mixer at medium speed about 3 minutes or until light and fluffy. Add egg, honey and vanilla; beat until well blended. Gradually add flour mixture, about ½ cup at a time; beat at low speed just until blended.

3 Drop dough by tablespoonfuls 2 inches apart onto prepared cookie sheets.

4 Bake 11 to 15 minutes or until cookies are puffed and golden. Cool on cookie sheets 5 minutes; remove to wire racks to cool completely.

lemony butter cookies

makes about 2½ dozen cookies

½ cup (1 stick) butter, softened

½ cup granulated sugar

1 egg

1½ cups all-purpose flour

2 tablespoons fresh lemon juice

1 teaspoon grated lemon peel

½ teaspoon baking powder

⅛ teaspoon salt

Sparkling sugar (optional)

1 Beat butter and granulated sugar in large bowl with electric mixer at medium speed about 2 minutes or until creamy. Add egg; beat until light and fluffy. Add flour, lemon juice, lemon peel, baking powder and salt; stir just until blended. Wrap dough with plastic wrap; refrigerate about 2 hours or until firm.

2 Preheat oven to 350°F. Roll out dough, a small portion at a time, to ¼-inch thickness on well-floured surface. (Keep remaining dough wrapped in refrigerator.)

3 Cut out dough with 3-inch fluted or round cookie cutter; place on ungreased cookie sheets. Sprinkle with sparkling sugar, if desired.

4 Bake 8 to 10 minutes or until edges are lightly browned. Cool on cookie sheets 1 minute; remove to wire racks to cool completely.

classic chocolate chip cookies

makes about 2 dozen cookies

1¼ cups all-purpose flour

½ teaspoon salt

½ teaspoon baking soda

½ cup (1 stick) butter, softened

½ cup granulated sugar

¼ cup packed brown sugar

1 egg

1 teaspoon vanilla

1 cup semisweet or bittersweet chocolate chips

Coarse salt or flaky sea salt (optional)

1 Preheat oven to 350°F. Line cookie sheets with parchment paper.

2 Combine flour, ½ teaspoon salt and baking soda in medium bowl; mix well. Beat butter, granulated sugar and brown sugar in large bowl with electric mixer at medium speed about 3 minutes or until light and fluffy. Add egg and vanilla; beat until well blended. Add flour mixture; beat at low speed just until blended. Stir in chocolate chips.

3 Drop dough by tablespoonfuls 2 inches apart onto prepared cookie sheets. Sprinkle with coarse salt, if desired.

4 Bake 10 to 12 minutes or until edges are lightly browned. Cool on cookie sheets 1 minute; remove to wire racks to cool completely.

tip: For the best flavor, wrap the dough with plastic wrap and refrigerate overnight or up to 2 days.

honey gingersnaps

makes 3½ dozen cookies

2 cups all-purpose flour
1 tablespoon ground ginger
2 teaspoons baking soda
⅛ teaspoon salt
⅛ teaspoon ground cloves
½ cup shortening

¼ cup (½ stick) butter, softened
1½ cups sugar, divided
¼ cup honey
1 egg
1 teaspoon vanilla

1 Preheat oven to 350°F. Line cookie sheets with parchment paper or spray with nonstick cooking spray.

2 Combine flour, ginger, baking soda, salt and cloves in medium bowl; mix well. Beat shortening and butter in large bowl with electric mixer at medium speed 1 to 2 minutes or until smooth. Gradually beat in 1 cup sugar until blended; beat at high speed 2 minutes or until light and fluffy. Add honey, egg and vanilla; beat at high speed until fluffy. Gradually add flour mixture; stir just until blended.

3 Place remaining ½ cup sugar in shallow bowl. Shape dough into 1-inch balls; roll in sugar to coat. Place 2 inches apart on prepared cookie sheets.

4 Bake 10 minutes or until cookies are golden brown. Cool on cookie sheets 5 minutes; remove to wire racks to cool completely.

refrigerator cookies

makes about 4 dozen cookies

1¾ cups all-purpose flour

¼ teaspoon baking soda

¼ teaspoon salt

½ cup granulated sugar

¼ cup light corn syrup

¼ cup (½ stick) butter, softened

1 egg

1 teaspoon vanilla

Decors and decorating sugars (optional)

1 Combine flour, baking soda and salt in medium bowl; mix well. Beat granulated sugar, corn syrup and butter in large bowl with electric mixer at medium speed until well blended. Add egg and vanilla; beat until smooth. Add flour mixture; beat at low speed just until blended.

2 Divide dough in half; shape each half into a log 1½ inches in diameter. Wrap with plastic wrap; freeze 1 hour.

3 Preheat oven to 350°F. Line baking sheets with parchment paper. Cut dough into ¼-inch-thick slices; place 1 inch apart on prepared cookie sheets. Sprinkle with decors, if desired.

4 Bake 8 to 10 minutes or until edges are golden brown. Remove to wire racks to cool completely.

variations: For chocolate cookies, add 2 tablespoons unsweetened cocoa powder to the flour mixture. For sugar-rimmed cookies, roll the logs of dough in colored sugar before freezing and slicing.

mini chocolate whoopie pies

makes about 2 dozen sandwich cookies

1¾ cups all-purpose flour

½ cup unsweetened Dutch process cocoa powder

¾ teaspoon baking powder

½ teaspoon baking soda

½ teaspoon salt

1 cup packed brown sugar

1 cup (2 sticks) butter, softened, divided

1 egg

1½ teaspoons vanilla, divided

1 cup milk

1 cup marshmallow creme

1 cup powdered sugar

1 Preheat oven to 350°F. Line cookie sheets with parchment paper.

2 Sift flour, cocoa, baking powder, baking soda and salt into medium bowl. Beat brown sugar and ½ cup butter in large bowl with electric mixer at medium-high speed about 3 minutes or until light and fluffy. Beat in egg and 1 teaspoon vanilla until well blended. Alternately add flour mixture and milk, beating at low speed after each addition until smooth and well blended.

3 Drop dough by heaping teaspoonfuls 2 inches apart onto prepared cookie sheets.

4 Bake 8 to 10 minutes or until cookies are puffed and tops spring back when lightly touched. Cool on cookie sheets 10 minutes; remove to wire racks to cool completely.

5 Meanwhile, prepare filling. Beat remaining ½ cup butter, ½ teaspoon vanilla, marshmallow creme and powdered sugar in large bowl with electric mixer at high speed 2 minutes or until light and fluffy. Pipe or spread heaping teaspoon filling onto flat side of half of cookies; top with remaining cookies.

pb and j thumbprint cookies

makes about 40 cookies

2 cups old-fashioned oats

1⅓ cups plus 1 tablespoon all-purpose flour

¾ teaspoon baking soda

½ teaspoon baking powder

½ teaspoon salt

1 cup packed brown sugar

¾ cup (1½ sticks) butter, softened

¼ cup granulated sugar

¼ cup chunky peanut butter

1 egg

1 tablespoon honey

1 teaspoon vanilla

½ cup chopped peanuts, unsalted or honey-roasted

½ cup grape jelly or favorite flavor

1 Preheat oven to 350°F. Line cookie sheets with parchment paper.

2 Combine oats, flour, baking soda, baking powder and salt in medium bowl; mix well. Beat brown sugar, butter and granulated sugar in large bowl with electric mixer at medium speed 2 minutes or until well blended. Beat at high speed 2 minutes or until light and fluffy. Add peanut butter, egg, honey and vanilla; beat at medium speed until well blended. Gradually add flour mixture; beat just until blended. Stir in peanuts.

3 Drop dough by rounded tablespoonfuls onto prepared cookie sheets.

4 Bake 10 minutes. Press center of each cookie with back of teaspoon to make slight indentation; fill with about ½ teaspoon jelly. Bake 4 to 6 minutes or until puffed and golden brown. Cool on cookie sheets 5 minutes; remove to wire racks to cool completely.

new england raisin spice cookies

makes about 5 dozen cookies

2¼ cups all-purpose flour

2 teaspoons baking soda

1 teaspoon salt

¾ teaspoon ground cinnamon

¼ teaspoon ground ginger

¼ teaspoon ground cloves

⅛ teaspoon ground allspice

1½ cups raisins

1 cup packed brown sugar

½ cup shortening

¼ cup (½ stick) butter, softened

1 egg

⅓ cup molasses

1 cup granulated sugar

1 Combine flour, baking soda, salt, cinnamon, ginger, cloves and allspice in medium bowl; mix well. Stir in raisins.

2 Beat brown sugar, shortening and butter in large bowl with electric mixer at medium speed 2 minutes or until creamy. Add egg and molasses; beat 2 minutes or until light and fluffy. Gradually add flour mixture; stir just until blended. Cover and refrigerate at least 2 hours.

3 Preheat oven to 350°F. Place granulated sugar in shallow bowl. Shape heaping tablespoonfuls of dough into balls; roll balls in granulated sugar to coat. Place 2 inches apart on ungreased cookie sheets.

4 Bake 8 minutes or until cookies are golden brown. Cool on cookie sheets 1 minute; remove to wire racks to cool completely.

chunky brownie cookies

makes about 4 dozen cookies

2 cups all-purpose flour

½ cup unsweetened Dutch process cocoa powder

1 teaspoon baking soda

¾ teaspoon salt

1 cup (2 sticks) butter, softened

1 cup packed brown sugar

½ cup granulated sugar

2 eggs

2 teaspoons vanilla

1 package (about 12 ounces) semisweet chocolate chunks

2 cups coarsely chopped walnuts or pecans

1 Preheat oven to 350°F. Combine flour, cocoa, baking soda and salt in medium bowl; mix well.

2 Beat butter, brown sugar and granulated sugar in large bowl with electric mixer at medium speed 3 minutes or until light and fluffy. Add eggs and vanilla; beat until well blended. Gradually add flour mixture; beat at low speed just until blended. Stir in chocolate chunks and walnuts.

3 Drop dough by heaping tablespoonfuls 2 inches apart onto ungreased cookie sheets; flatten slightly.

4 Bake 8 to 10 minutes or until set. Cool on cookie sheets 2 minutes; remove to wire racks to cool completely.

snickerdoodles

1⅓ cups all-purpose flour

2 teaspoons ground cinnamon, divided

1 teaspoon cream of tartar

½ teaspoon baking soda

½ teaspoon salt

¾ cup plus 2 tablespoons sugar, divided

½ cup (1 stick) butter, softened

1 egg

1 Preheat oven to 375°F. Line cookie sheets with parchment paper.

2 Combine flour, 1 teaspoon cinnamon, cream of tartar, baking soda and salt in medium bowl; mix well.

3 Beat ¾ cup sugar and butter in large bowl with electric mixer at medium speed about 2 minutes or until creamy. Beat in egg until blended. Gradually add flour mixture; beat at low speed until stiff dough forms.

4 Combine remaining 2 tablespoons sugar and 1 teaspoon cinnamon in small bowl. Roll dough into 1-inch balls; roll balls in cinnamon-sugar to coat. Place 2 inches apart on prepared cookie sheets.

5 Bake 10 minutes or until set. Remove to wire racks to cool completely.

linzer sandwich cookies

makes about 2 dozen sandwich cookies

1⅔ cups all-purpose flour

¼ teaspoon baking powder

¼ teaspoon salt

¾ cup granulated sugar

½ cup (1 stick) butter, softened

1 egg

1 teaspoon vanilla

Powdered sugar (optional)

Seedless red raspberry jam

1 Combine flour, baking powder and salt in medium bowl; mix well. Beat granulated sugar and butter in large bowl with electric mixer at medium speed about 3 minutes or until light and fluffy. Beat in egg and vanilla until blended. Gradually add flour mixture; beat at low speed just until dough forms. Divide dough in half. Wrap each half with plastic wrap; refrigerate 2 hours or until firm.

2 Preheat oven to 375°F. Roll out half of dough to ³⁄₁₆-inch thickness on lightly floured surface. Cut out circles with 1½-inch floured scalloped or plain round cookie cutters. (If dough becomes too soft, refrigerate several minutes before continuing.) Place cutouts 2 inches apart on ungreased cookie sheets.

3 Roll out remaining half of dough and cut out circles. Cut 1-inch centers of different shapes from circles. Place 2 inches apart on ungreased cookie sheets.

4 Bake 7 to 9 minutes or until edges are lightly browned. Cool on cookie sheets 2 minutes; remove to wire racks to cool completely.

5 Sprinkle powdered sugar over cookies with holes, if desired. Spread jam on flat sides of whole cookies; top with sugar-dusted cookies.

chocolate chip skillet cookie

makes 8 servings

1¾ cups all-purpose flour	2 eggs
1 teaspoon baking soda	1 teaspoon vanilla
1 teaspoon salt	1 package (12 ounces) semisweet chocolate chips
¾ cup (1½ sticks) butter, softened	Sea salt (optional)
¾ cup packed brown sugar	Ice cream (optional)
½ cup granulated sugar	

1 Preheat oven to 350°F. Combine flour, baking soda and 1 teaspoon salt in medium bowl; mix well.

2 Beat butter, brown sugar and granulated sugar in large bowl with electric mixer at medium speed about 2 minutes or until creamy. Add eggs and vanilla; beat until well blended. Gradually add in flour mixture; beat at low speed just until blended. Stir in chocolate chips.

3 Press batter evenly into well-seasoned* large (10-inch) cast iron skillet. Sprinkle lightly with sea salt, if desired.

4 Bake 35 minutes or until top and edges are golden brown but cookie is still soft in center. Cool on wire rack 10 minutes before cutting into wedges. Serve warm with ice cream, if desired.

*If skillet is not well seasoned, brush lightly with melted butter or vegetable oil.

BROWNIES & BARS

fruit and pecan brownies

makes 16 brownies

2 ounces unsweetened chocolate

1 cup sugar

½ cup (1 stick) butter, softened

2 eggs

1 teaspoon vanilla

½ cup all-purpose flour

1 cup chopped dried mixed fruit

1 cup coarsely chopped pecans, divided

1 cup (6 ounces) semisweet chocolate chips, divided

1 Preheat oven to 350°F. Spray 8-inch square baking pan with nonstick cooking spray.

2 Melt unsweetened chocolate in top of double boiler over hot, not boiling, water. Remove from heat; cool slightly.

3 Beat sugar and butter in large bowl with electric mixer at medium speed about 3 minutes or until light and fluffy. Add eggs, one at a time, beating well after each addition. Add chocolate and vanilla; beat until well blended. Stir in flour, fruit, ½ cup pecans and ½ cup chocolate chips just until blended. Spread batter evenly in prepared pan; sprinkle with remaining ½ cup pecans and ½ cup chocolate chips.

4 Bake 25 to 30 minutes or just until center feels firm. Remove to wire rack; cover loosely with foil. Cool completely in pan on wire rack.

easy celebration brownies

makes 2 to 3 dozen brownies

1 cup (2 sticks) butter

8 ounces semisweet baking chocolate, coarsely chopped

1 cup sugar

4 eggs

1 teaspoon vanilla

1 teaspoon salt

1¼ cups all-purpose flour

1 cup dark or semisweet chocolate chips

Chocolate Glaze (optional, recipe follows)

1 container (about 2 ounces) rainbow nonpareils (optional)

1 Preheat oven to 350°F. Spray 13x9-inch baking pan with nonstick cooking spray or line with parchment paper.

2 Heat butter and chopped chocolate in large heavy saucepan over low-heat; stir until melted and smooth. Remove from heat; stir in sugar until blended. Add eggs, one at a time, stirring until well blended after each addition. Stir in vanilla and salt. Add flour and 1 cup chocolate chips; stir just until blended. Spread batter evenly in prepared pan.

3 Bake 22 to 25 minutes or until center is set and toothpick inserted into center comes out clean. Cool completely in pan on wire rack.

4 Prepare Chocolate Glaze, if desired; spread evenly over brownies. Top with nonpareils.

chocolate glaze: Heat ¼ cup whipping cream in small saucepan over medium-low heat until bubbles appear around edge of pan. Remove from heat; add 1 cup dark or semisweet chocolate chips. Let stand 1 minute; whisk until smooth and well blended.

mocha fudge brownies

makes 16 brownies

3 ounces semisweet chocolate

¾ cup sugar

½ cup (1 stick) butter, softened

2 eggs

2 teaspoons instant espresso powder

1 teaspoon vanilla

½ cup all-purpose flour

½ cup chopped toasted almonds*

1 cup milk chocolate chips, divided

*To toast almonds, spread on ungreased baking sheet. Bake in preheated 350°F oven 5 to 7 minutes or until lightly browned, stirring occasionally.

1 Preheat oven to 350°F. Spray 8-inch square baking pan with nonstick cooking spray.

2 Melt semisweet chocolate in top of double boiler over hot, not boiling, water. Remove from heat; cool slightly.

3 Beat sugar and butter in medium bowl with electric mixer at medium speed about 3 minutes or until light and fluffy. Add eggs, one at a time, beating until blended after each addition. Add melted chocolate, espresso powder and vanilla; beat until well blended. Add flour, almonds and ½ cup chocolate chips; stir just until blended. Spread batter in prepared pan.

4 Bake 25 minutes or until set. Sprinkle with remaining ½ cup chocolate chips. Let stand until melted; spread chocolate evenly over brownies. Cool completely in pan on wire rack.

coconut blondies

makes 2 to 3 dozen bars

2 cups all-purpose flour

1½ tablespoons baking powder

½ teaspoon salt

1⅔ cups packed brown sugar

1 cup chopped toasted pecans*

¾ cup lightly packed flaked coconut

¾ cup (1½ sticks) butter, melted

2 eggs, lightly beaten

1 teaspoon vanilla

*To toast pecans, spread on baking sheet. Bake in preheated 350°F oven 8 to 10 minutes or until golden brown, stirring frequently. Cool before using.

1 Preheat oven to 350°F. Spray 13×9-inch baking pan with nonstick cooking spray.

2 Combine flour, baking powder and salt in large bowl; mix well. Add brown sugar, pecans and coconut; stir until well blended. Make well in center of dry ingredients. Add butter, eggs and vanilla; stir just until moistened. Spread batter in prepared pan.

3 Bake 25 minutes or until toothpick inserted into center comes out clean. Cool completely in pan on wire rack.

classic layered bars

makes 2 to 3 dozen bars

⅓ cup butter

1 cup graham cracker crumbs

½ cup old-fashioned or quick oats

1 can (14 ounces) sweetened
    condensed milk

1 cup unsweetened shredded
    coconut

¾ cup semisweet chocolate chips

¾ cup raisins

1 cup coarsely chopped pecans

1 Preheat oven to 350°F. Melt butter in 13×9-inch baking pan. Remove from oven.

2 Sprinkle graham cracker crumbs and oats evenly over butter; press down with fork.
Drizzle condensed milk over oats; layer with coconut, chocolate chips, raisins and
pecans.

3 Bake 25 to 30 minutes or until lightly browned. Cool in pan on wire rack 5 minutes;
cut into bars. Cool completely in pan on wire rack.

cherry cheesecake swirl bars

makes 16 bars

crust

1⅔ cups crushed graham cracker crumbs (about 25 graham cracker squares)

6 tablespoons (¾ stick) butter, melted

3 tablespoons sugar

cheesecake

2 packages (8 ounces each) cream cheese, softened

½ cup sugar

2 eggs

1 egg yolk

⅓ cup sour cream

1 tablespoon all-purpose flour

½ teaspoon almond extract

3 tablespoons strained melted cherry preserves

1 Preheat oven to 325°F. Combine graham cracker crumbs, butter and 3 tablespoons sugar in medium bowl; mix well. Press mixture into bottom of 9-inch square baking pan.

2 Bake 8 minutes or until set but not browned. Cool completely on wire rack.

3 Beat cream cheese in medium bowl with electric mixer at medium speed 2 minutes or until smooth and creamy. Add ½ cup sugar; beat until smooth. Add eggs, egg yolk, sour cream, flour and almond extract; beat until well blended. Spread evenly over cooled crust.

4 Drizzle melted preserves in zigzag pattern over cheesecake batter. Drag tip of knife through jam and batter to make swirls.

5 Place cheesecake in pan in 13×9-inch baking dish. Add water to baking dish to come halfway up sides of cheesecake pan. Bake 45 minutes or until knife inserted 1 inch from edge comes out clean. Cool completely in pan on wire rack. Refrigerate 2 hours or until cold.

variation: Substitute any seedless jam for the cherry preserves and use vanilla instead of almond extract.

pumpkin pecan crunch bars

makes 2 to 3 dozen bars

1½ cups all-purpose flour, divided

½ cup packed brown sugar

¼ cup (½ stick) butter, cut into small pieces

1 cup coarsely chopped pecans

1½ teaspoons baking powder

1 teaspoon ground cinnamon

¼ teaspoon salt

¼ teaspoon baking soda

⅛ teaspoon ground ginger

1 cup granulated sugar

1 cup canned pumpkin

½ cup vegetable oil

2 eggs

2 tablespoons butter, melted

1 Preheat oven to 350°F. Spray 13×9-inch baking pan with nonstick cooking spray or line pan with foil.

2 For topping, combine ½ cup flour and brown sugar in medium bowl. Cut in ¼ cup butter with pastry blender or two knives until mixture resembles coarse crumbs. Stir in pecans.

3 Combine remaining 1 cup flour, baking powder, cinnamon, salt, baking soda and ginger in medium bowl; mix well. Beat granulated sugar, pumpkin, oil, eggs and melted butter in large bowl with electric mixer at medium speed until well blended. Gradually add flour mixture; beat until blended. Spread batter in prepared pan; sprinkle with topping.

4 Bake 35 minutes or until toothpick inserted into center comes out clean. Cool completely in pan on wire rack.

chocolate pecan bars

makes 2 to 3 dozen bars

crust

1⅓ cups all-purpose flour

½ cup (1 stick) butter, softened

¼ cup packed brown sugar

½ teaspoon salt

topping

¾ cup light corn syrup

3 eggs, lightly beaten

2 tablespoons butter, melted and cooled

½ teaspoon vanilla

½ teaspoon almond extract

¾ cup milk chocolate chips

¾ cup semisweet chocolate chips

¾ cup chopped pecans, toasted*

¾ cup granulated sugar

*To toast pecans, spread on baking sheet. Bake in preheated 350°F oven 5 to 7 minutes or until lightly browned and fragrant, stirring frequently.

1 Preheat oven to 350°F. Spray 13×9-inch baking pan with nonstick cooking spray.

2 For crust, combine flour, ½ cup softened butter, brown sugar and salt in medium bowl; mix with fork until crumbly. Press into bottom of prepared pan. Bake 12 to 15 minutes or until lightly browned. Cool on wire rack 10 minutes.

3 Meanwhile, for topping, combine corn syrup, eggs, 2 tablespoons melted butter, vanilla and almond extract in large bowl; stir with fork until well blended (do not beat). Fold in chocolate chips, pecans and granulated sugar until blended. Pour over baked crust.

4 Bake 25 to 30 minutes or until toothpick inserted into center comes out clean. Cool completely in pan on wire rack.

tip: To make measuring corn syrup easier, spray the inside of the measuring cup with nonstick cooking spray before using—the corn syrup will slide right out and won't stick to the cup.

berry crumble bars

makes 16 bars

3 cups all-purpose flour

½ cup plus ⅓ cup granulated sugar, divided

½ cup packed brown sugar

1 teaspoon baking powder

1 teaspoon grated lemon peel

½ teaspoon salt

1 cup (2 sticks) cold butter, cut into small pieces

1 egg, beaten

2½ tablespoons lemon juice

1 tablespoon cornstarch

1 package (16 ounces) frozen mixed berries (do not thaw)

1 Preheat oven to 375°F. Spray 9-inch square baking pan with nonstick cooking spray or line with parchment paper and spray paper with cooking spray.

2 Combine flour, ½ cup granulated sugar, brown sugar, baking powder, lemon peel and salt in large bowl; mix well. Add butter and egg; mix with pastry blender or fingertips until crumbly dough forms. Pat one third of dough into bottom of prepared pan.

3 Combine remaining ⅓ cup granulated sugar, lemon juice and cornstarch in medium bowl; mix well. Add berries, stir gently until well blended and berries are completely coated with sugar mixture. Spread evenly over crust. Top with remaining dough, crumbling into large pieces over fruit.

4 Bake 45 to 50 minutes or until top is golden brown. Cool in pan on wire rack. (Refrigerating bars for several hours will make them easier to cut.)

double chocolate dream bars

makes 2 to 3 dozen bars

2¼ cups all-purpose flour, divided

1 cup (2 sticks) butter, softened

¾ cup powdered sugar, plus additional for garnish

⅓ cup unsweetened cocoa powder

½ teaspoon salt

2 cups granulated sugar

4 eggs

4 ounces unsweetened chocolate, melted

1 Preheat oven to 350°F. Line 13×9-inch baking pan with parchment paper.

2 Beat 2 cups flour, butter, ¾ cup powdered sugar, cocoa and salt in large bowl with electric mixer at low speed until blended. Beat at medium speed until well blended and stiff dough forms. Press firmly into bottom of prepared pan. Bake 15 to 20 minutes or just until set.

3 Meanwhile, combine remaining ¼ cup flour and granulated sugar in large bowl. Add eggs and melted chocolate; beat with electric mixer at medium-high speed until well blended. Pour over crust.

4 Bake 25 minutes or until center is firm to the touch. Cool completely in pan on wire rack. Sprinkle with additional powdered sugar, if desired.

southern caramel apple bars

makes 2 to 3 dozen bars

2 cups all-purpose flour

1 teaspoon salt

½ teaspoon baking powder

½ teaspoon baking soda

⅔ cup butter

¾ cup packed brown sugar

½ cup granulated sugar

1 egg

1 teaspoon vanilla

4 Granny Smith apples, peeled and coarsely chopped

½ cup pecans, chopped

24 caramel candies, unwrapped

2 tablespoons milk

1 Preheat oven to 350°F. Spray 13×9-inch baking pan with nonstick cooking spray.

2 Combine flour, salt, baking powder and baking soda in medium bowl; mix well. Melt butter in medium saucepan over medium heat. Remove from heat; stir in brown sugar and granulated sugar. Add egg and vanilla; stir until well blended. Add flour mixture; stir until blended. Press into bottom of prepared pan; top with apples.

3 Bake 40 to 45 minutes or until edges are browned and pulling away from sides of pan. Cool completely in pan on wire rack.

4 Toast pecans in medium nonstick skillet over medium-high heat 2 minutes or until fragrant, stirring frequently. Remove to small bowl. Wipe out skillet with paper towel. Heat caramels and milk in same skillet over medium-low heat until melted and smooth, stirring constantly.

5 Drizzle caramel sauce over cooled apple bars; sprinkle with pecans. Let stand 30 minutes before cutting.

lemon squares

makes 2 to 3 dozen bars

crust

- 1 cup (2 sticks) butter, softened
- ½ cup granulated sugar
- ½ teaspoon salt
- 2 cups all-purpose flour

filling

- 3 cups granulated sugar
- 1 cup all-purpose flour
- 4 eggs plus 2 egg yolks, at room temperature
- ⅔ cup fresh lemon juice
- 2 tablespoons grated lemon peel
- ½ teaspoon baking powder
- Powdered sugar

1. For crust, beat butter, ½ cup granulated sugar and salt in large bowl with electric mixer at medium speed until light and fluffy. Add 2 cups flour; beat at low speed just until blended.

2. Press dough into 13×9-inch baking pan, building edges up ½ inch on all sides. Refrigerate 20 minutes or until slightly firm. Preheat oven to 350°F.

3. Bake 15 to 20 minutes or until very lightly browned. Cool on wire rack 10 minutes while preparing filling.

4. For filling, whisk 3 cups granulated sugar, 1 cup flour, eggs and egg yolks, lemon juice, lemon peel and baking powder in large bowl until well blended. Pour over crust.

5. Bake 30 to 35 minutes until filling is set. Cool completely in pan on wire rack. Cut into bars; sprinkle with powdered sugar.

nutty chocolate oat bars

makes 2 to 3 dozen bars

1 cup all-purpose flour
1 cup old-fashioned oats
¾ cup packed brown sugar
½ cup (1 stick) butter, softened

1 can (14 ounces) sweetened condensed milk
1 cup chopped walnuts or pecans
1 cup semisweet chocolate chips

1 Preheat oven to 350°F. Combine flour, oats, brown sugar and butter in large bowl; stir until crumbly.

2 Reserve ½ cup oat mixture for topping. Press remaining mixture firmly into bottom of 13×9-inch baking pan.

3 Bake 10 minutes. Remove pan from oven; pour condensed milk evenly over crust. Sprinkle with walnuts and chocolate chips. Top with reserved oat mixture; press down firmly.

4 Bake 25 minutes or until top is lightly browned. Cool completely in pan on wire rack.

QUICK BREADS & MUFFINS

cranberry pumpkin nut bread

makes 1 loaf

2 cups all-purpose flour

2 teaspoons pumpkin pie spice

1 teaspoon baking powder

½ teaspoon baking soda

½ teaspoon salt

1 cup canned pumpkin

¾ cup granulated sugar

½ cup packed brown sugar

2 eggs

⅓ cup vegetable or canola oil

1 cup chopped dried cranberries

¾ cup chopped macadamia nuts, toasted*

*To toast macadamia nuts, spread on ungreased baking sheet. Bake in 350°F oven 8 to 10 minutes or until lightly browned, stirring occasionally.

1 Preheat oven to 350°F. Spray 9×5-inch loaf pan with nonstick cooking spray.

2 Combine flour, pumpkin pie spice, baking powder, baking soda and salt in large bowl; mix well. Whisk pumpkin, granulated sugar, brown sugar, eggs and oil in medium bowl until well blended. Add to flour mixture; stir just until dry ingredients are moistened. Stir in cranberries and nuts. Pour batter into prepared pan.

3 Bake 45 to 50 minutes or until toothpick inserted into center comes out clean. Cool in pan 15 minutes; remove to wire rack to cool completely.

irish soda bread

makes 1 loaf

2½ cups all-purpose flour

1¼ cups whole wheat flour

1 cup currants

¼ cup sugar

4 teaspoons baking powder

2 teaspoons caraway seeds (optional)

1 teaspoon salt

½ teaspoon baking soda

½ cup (1 stick) butter, cut into small pieces

1⅓ to 1½ cups buttermilk

1 Preheat oven to 350°F. Line baking sheet with parchment paper or spray with nonstick cooking spray.

2 Combine all-purpose flour, whole wheat flour, currants, sugar, baking powder, caraway seeds, if desired, salt and baking soda in large bowl; mix well.

3 Cut in butter with pastry blender or two knives until mixture resembles coarse crumbs. Add buttermilk; stir until slightly sticky dough forms. Transfer dough to prepared baking sheet; shape into 8-inch round.

4 Bake 50 to 60 minutes or until bread is golden brown and crust is firm. Cool on baking sheet 10 minutes; remove to wire rack to cool completely.

bacon-jalapeño corn bread

makes 9 to 12 servings

4 slices bacon

¼ cup minced green onions

2 jalapeño peppers,* seeded and minced

1 cup all-purpose flour

1 cup yellow cornmeal

2½ teaspoons baking powder

¾ teaspoon salt

½ teaspoon baking soda

¾ cup plain yogurt

1 egg

¾ cup milk

¼ cup (½ stick) butter, melted

½ cup (2 ounces) shredded Cheddar cheese

*Jalapeño peppers can sting and irritate the skin, so wear rubber gloves when handling peppers and do not touch your eyes.

1 Preheat oven to 400°F.

2 Cook bacon in large skillet over medium heat until crisp. Drain on paper towel-lined plate. Pour 2 tablespoons drippings into 9-inch square baking pan or cast iron skillet.

3 Crumble bacon into small bowl; stir in green onions and jalapeños. Combine flour, cornmeal, baking powder, salt and baking soda in large bowl; mix well.

4 Whisk yogurt and egg in medium bowl until smooth. Add milk and butter; whisk until well blended. Add to flour mixture; stir just until dry ingredients are moistened. Stir in bacon mixture. Pour batter into prepared pan; sprinkle with cheese.

5 Bake 20 to 25 minutes or until toothpick inserted into center comes out clean. Cut into squares or wedges.

blueberry-apricot streusel bread

makes 1 loaf

2 cups plus 2 tablespoons all-purpose flour, divided

1 cup plus 2 tablespoons sugar, divided

¾ cup chopped dried apricots

¾ cup chopped dried blueberries

1 teaspoon baking powder

½ teaspoon baking soda

½ teaspoon salt

¾ cup buttermilk

½ cup (1 stick) butter, melted and cooled

1 egg

1 teaspoon vanilla

½ teaspoon almond extract

2 tablespoons chopped sliced almonds

1 teaspoon ground cinnamon

2 tablespoons cold butter, cut into small pieces

1 Preheat oven to 350°F. Spray 9×5-inch loaf pan with nonstick cooking spray.

2 Combine 2 cups flour, 1 cup sugar, apricots, blueberries, baking powder, baking soda and salt in large bowl; mix well. Whisk buttermilk, melted butter, egg, vanilla and almond extract in medium bowl until well blended. Add to flour mixture; stir just until dry ingredients are moistened. Spread batter evenly in prepared pan.

3 Combine remaining 2 tablespoons flour, 2 tablespoons sugar, almonds and cinnamon in small bowl. Add cold butter; mix with fork until crumbly. Sprinkle over batter.

4 Bake 55 to 65 minutes or until toothpick inserted into center comes out clean. Cool in pan 15 minutes; remove to wire rack to cool completely.

marbled banana bread

makes 1 loaf

2 cups all-purpose flour

1 teaspoon baking soda

1 teaspoon salt

1 cup sugar

6 tablespoons (¾ stick) butter, softened

1½ cups mashed ripe bananas (about 3 medium)

2 eggs

½ cup sour cream

1 teaspoon vanilla

¾ cup semisweet chocolate chips

1 Preheat oven to 350°F. Spray 9×5-inch loaf pan with nonstick cooking spray or line with parchment paper.

2 Combine flour, baking soda and salt in medium bowl; mix well. Beat sugar and butter in large bowl with wooden spoon until well blended. Add bananas, eggs, sour cream and vanilla; stir until blended. Add flour mixture; stir just until dry ingredients are moistened.

3 Place chocolate chips in medium microwavable bowl; microwave at HIGH 1 minute. Stir until chocolate is melted and smooth; let cool 3 minutes. Add 1 cup batter to melted chocolate; stir until blended. Spoon plain and chocolate batters alternately into prepared pan; swirl batters together with knife or wooden skewer.

4 Bake 1 hour to 1 hour and 5 minutes or until toothpick inserted into center comes out clean. Cool in pan 10 minutes; remove to wire rack to cool completely.

harvest quick bread

makes 1 loaf

1 cup all-purpose flour

1 cup whole wheat flour

½ cup packed brown sugar

¼ cup granulated sugar

1½ teaspoons baking powder

½ teaspoon baking soda

½ teaspoon ground cinnamon

½ teaspoon salt

1 egg

1 cup milk

¼ cup (½ stick) butter, melted

¾ cup dried cranberries

½ cup chopped walnuts

1 Preheat oven to 350°F. Spray 9×5-inch loaf pan with nonstick cooking spray.

2 Combine all-purpose flour, whole wheat flour, brown sugar, granulated sugar, baking powder, baking soda, cinnamon and salt in medium bowl; mix well.

3 Whisk egg in large bowl. Add milk and butter; whisk until well blended. Gradually add flour mixture; stir just until dry ingredients are moistened. Stir in cranberries and walnuts just until combined. Pour batter into prepared pan.

4 Bake 45 to 50 minutes or until toothpick inserted into center comes out clean. Cool in pan 10 minutes; remove to wire rack to cool completely.

apple butter spice muffins

makes 12 muffins

½ cup sugar

1 teaspoon ground cinnamon

¼ teaspoon ground nutmeg

⅛ teaspoon ground allspice

½ cup pecans or walnuts, chopped

2 cups all-purpose flour

2 teaspoons baking powder

¼ teaspoon salt

1 cup milk

¼ cup vegetable oil

1 egg

¼ cup apple butter

1 Preheat oven to 400°F. Line 12 standard (2½-inch) muffin cups with paper baking cups or spray with nonstick cooking spray.

2 Combine sugar, cinnamon, nutmeg and allspice in large bowl. Remove 2 tablespoons sugar mixture to small bowl; toss with pecans until coated. Add flour, baking powder and salt to remaining sugar mixture.

3 Whisk milk, oil and egg in medium bowl until well blended. Add to flour mixture; stir just until dry ingredients are moistened. Spoon 1 tablespoon batter into each prepared muffin cup. Top with 1 teaspoon apple butter; spoon remaining batter evenly over apple butter. Sprinkle with pecan mixture.

4 Bake 20 to 25 minutes or until golden brown and toothpick inserted into centers comes out clean. Remove to wire rack to cool 10 minutes. Serve warm or cool completely.

lemon-glazed zucchini muffins

makes 12 muffins

2 cups all-purpose flour

⅔ cup granulated sugar

1 tablespoon baking powder

1 teaspoon salt

½ teaspoon ground nutmeg

2 teaspoons grated lemon peel

½ cup chopped walnuts, pecans or hazelnuts

½ cup dried fruit bits or golden raisins

½ cup milk

⅓ cup vegetable oil

2 eggs

1 cup packed shredded zucchini, undrained

1 to 1½ teaspoons lemon juice

¼ cup powdered sugar

1 Preheat oven to 400°F. Spray 12 standard (2½-inch) muffin cups with nonstick cooking spray or line with paper baking cups.

2 Combine flour, granulated sugar, baking powder, salt, nutmeg and lemon peel in large bowl; stir in nuts and fruit. Whisk milk, oil and eggs in small bowl until blended. Add to flour mixture with zucchini; stir just until dry ingredients are moistened. Spoon batter evenly into prepared muffin cups.

3 Bake 20 to 25 minutes or until toothpick inserted into centers comes out clean. Remove to wire rack to cool 5 minutes.

4 Meanwhile, stir lemon juice into powdered sugar in small bowl until smooth. Drizzle glaze over warm muffins.

jumbo streusel-topped raspberry muffins

makes 6 jumbo muffins

2¼ cups all-purpose flour, divided

¼ cup packed brown sugar

2 tablespoons cold butter, cut into small pieces

¾ cup granulated sugar

2 teaspoons baking powder

½ teaspoon baking soda

½ teaspoon salt

½ teaspoon grated lemon peel

¾ cup plus 2 tablespoons milk

⅓ cup butter, melted

1 egg, beaten

2 cups fresh or frozen raspberries (do not thaw)

1 Preheat oven to 350°F. Spray 6 jumbo (3½-inch) muffin cups with nonstick cooking spray.

2 For topping, combine ¼ cup flour and brown sugar in small bowl. Cut in 2 tablespoons cold butter with pastry blender or two knives until coarse crumbs form.

3 Reserve ¼ cup flour in medium bowl. Combine remaining 1¾ cups flour, granulated sugar, baking powder, baking soda, salt and lemon peel in large bowl; mix well. Whisk milk, ⅓ cup melted butter and egg in small bowl until blended. Add to flour mixture; stir just until dry ingredients are moistened.

4 Add raspberries to reserved flour; stir gently to coat. Gently fold raspberries into muffin batter. Spoon batter into prepared muffin cups, filling three-fourths full. Sprinkle with topping.

5 Bake 25 to 30 minutes or until toothpick inserted into centers comes out clean. Cool in pan 2 minutes; remove to wire rack. Serve warm or at room temperature.

variation: For smaller muffins, spoon batter into 12 standard (2½-inch) greased or paper-lined muffin cups. Bake at 350°F 21 to 24 minutes or until toothpick inserted into centers comes out clean.

banana peanut butter chip muffins

makes 15 muffins

2 cups all-purpose flour

¾ cup sugar

2 teaspoons baking powder

½ teaspoon baking soda

¼ teaspoon salt

1 cup mashed ripe bananas
  (about 2 large)

½ cup (1 stick) butter, melted

2 eggs, beaten

⅓ cup buttermilk

1½ teaspoons vanilla

1 cup peanut butter chips

½ cup chopped peanuts

1 Preheat oven to 375°F. Line 15 standard (2½-inch) muffins cups with paper baking cups or spray with nonstick cooking spray.

2 Combine flour, sugar, baking powder, baking soda and salt in large bowl; mix well. Whisk bananas, butter, eggs, buttermilk and vanilla in medium bowl until well blended. Add to flour mixture; stir just until blended. Gently fold in peanut butter chips. Spoon batter into prepared muffin cups, filling three-fourths full. Sprinkle with chopped peanuts.

3 Bake 20 minutes or until toothpick inserted into centers comes out clean. Cool in pans 2 minutes; remove to wire racks to cool completely.

cornmeal pecan muffins

makes 12 muffins

¼ cup pecans

1 cup yellow cornmeal

¾ cup all-purpose flour

⅓ cup sugar

2 teaspoons baking powder

½ teaspoon baking soda

¼ teaspoon salt

1¼ cups buttermilk*

2 eggs

¼ cup vegetable oil

If buttermilk is unavailable, substitute 3½ teaspoons vinegar or lemon juice plus enough milk to equal 1¼ cups. Stir; let stand 5 minutes.

1 Preheat oven to 350°F. Spray 12 standard (2½-inch) muffin cups with nonstick cooking spray.

2 Spread pecans on ungreased baking sheet. Bake 8 to 10 minutes or until golden brown, stirring frequently. Remove to plate to cool. *Increase oven temperature to 375°F.*

3 Combine cornmeal, flour, sugar, baking powder, baking soda and salt in large bowl; mix well. Whisk buttermilk, eggs and oil in medium bowl until blended. Add to cornmeal mixture; stir just until dry ingredients are moistened. Stir in pecans. Spoon batter evenly into prepared muffin cups.

4 Bake 15 to 18 minutes or until tops are lightly browned. Cool in pan 5 minutes; remove to wire rack. Serve warm or cool completely.

pumpkin chocolate chip muffins

makes 18 muffins

2½ cups all-purpose flour

1 tablespoon baking powder

1½ teaspoons pumpkin pie spice*

½ teaspoon salt

1 cup canned pumpkin

1 cup packed brown sugar

¾ cup milk

6 tablespoons (¾ stick) butter, melted

2 eggs

1 cup semisweet chocolate chips

½ cup chopped walnuts

Or substitute ¾ teaspoon ground cinnamon, ½ teaspoon ground ginger and ¼ teaspoon each ground allspice and ground nutmeg.

1 Preheat oven to 400°F. Line 18 standard (2½-inch) muffin cups with paper baking cups or spray with nonstick cooking spray.

2 Combine flour, baking powder, pumpkin pie spice and salt in large bowl; mix well. Whisk pumpkin, brown sugar, milk, butter and eggs in medium bowl until well blended. Add pumpkin mixture, chocolate chips and walnuts to flour mixture; stir just until dry ingredients are moistened. Spoon evenly into prepared muffin cups, filling two-thirds full.

3 Bake 15 minutes or until toothpick inserted into centers comes out clean. Cool in pans 10 minutes; remove to wire racks to cool completely.

baked birthday cake doughnuts

makes 12 doughnuts

1 cup all-purpose flour

½ cup granulated sugar

½ cup multicolored sprinkles, divided

2 tablespoons cornstarch

1½ teaspoons baking powder

½ teaspoon baking soda

½ teaspoon salt

½ cup buttermilk

¼ cup orange juice

1 egg

2 tablespoons butter, melted

½ teaspoon vanilla

3 tablespoons butter

1½ cups powdered sugar

1½ tablespoons milk or cream

1 Preheat oven to 425°F. Spray 12 cavities of doughnut pan with nonstick cooking spray.

2 Combine flour, granulated sugar, ¼ cup sprinkles, cornstarch, baking powder, baking soda and salt in large bowl; mix well. Whisk buttermilk, orange juice, egg, 2 tablespoons melted butter and vanilla in medium bowl until well blended. Add to flour mixture; stir until smooth and well blended.

3 Spoon batter into large resealable food storage bag. Cut small corner from bag; pipe batter evenly into prepared cups, filling half full.

4 Bake 7 to 9 minutes or until doughnuts are puffed and golden brown. Cool in pan 3 to 5 minutes; remove to wire rack to cool completely.

5 For glaze, melt 3 tablespoons butter in small saucepan over low heat. Whisk in powdered sugar and milk; cook 1 minute or until mixture is smooth. Working quickly, dip tops of doughnuts into glaze; place on wire rack and immediately sprinkle with remaining ¼ cup sprinkles. If glaze hardens, rewarm briefly over low heat.

cheddar biscuits

2 cups all-purpose flour

1 tablespoon sugar

1 tablespoon baking powder

2¼ teaspoons garlic powder, divided

¾ teaspoon plus pinch of salt, divided

1 cup whole milk

½ cup (1 stick) plus 3 tablespoons butter, melted, divided

2 cups (8 ounces) shredded Cheddar cheese

½ teaspoon dried parsley flakes

1 Preheat oven to 450°F. Line baking sheet with parchment paper.

2 Combine flour, sugar, baking powder, 2 teaspoons garlic powder and ¾ teaspoon salt in large bowl; mix well. Add milk and ½ cup melted butter; stir just until dry ingredients are moistened. Stir in cheese just until blended. Drop scant ¼ cupfuls of dough about 1½ inches apart onto prepared baking sheet.

3 Bake 10 to 12 minutes or until golden brown.

4 Meanwhile, combine remaining 3 tablespoons melted butter, ¼ teaspoon garlic powder, pinch of salt and parsley flakes in small bowl; brush over biscuits immediately after removing from oven. Serve warm.

sweet cherry biscuits

makes about 10 biscuits

2 cups all-purpose flour

¼ cup sugar

4 teaspoons baking powder

½ teaspoon salt

½ teaspoon dried rosemary (optional)

½ cup (1 stick) cold butter, cut into small pieces

¾ cup milk

½ cup dried sweetened cherries, chopped

1 Preheat oven to 425°F.

2 Combine flour, sugar, baking powder, salt and rosemary, if desired, in large bowl; mix well. Cut in butter with pastry blender or two knives until mixture forms small crumbs. Stir in milk to form sticky batter. Stir in cherries.

3 Turn out dough onto floured surface; pat to 1-inch thickness. Cut out biscuits with 3-inch biscuit cutter. Place 1 inch apart on ungreased baking sheet.

4 Bake 15 minutes or until golden brown. Remove to wire rack to cool 5 minutes. Serve warm.

yogurt chive biscuits

makes 12 biscuits

2 cups all-purpose flour

1 tablespoon sugar

2 teaspoons baking powder

½ teaspoon baking soda

½ teaspoon salt

¼ teaspoon dried oregano

¼ cup (½ stick) cold butter, cut into small pieces

⅔ cup plain Greek yogurt

½ cup milk

¼ cup sour cream

½ cup finely chopped fresh chives

1 Preheat oven to 400°F. Line baking sheet with parchment paper or spray with nonstick cooking spray.

2 Combine flour, sugar, baking powder, baking soda, salt and oregano in large bowl; mix well. Cut in butter with pastry blender or two knives until mixture resembles coarse crumbs. Add yogurt, milk and sour cream; stir gently to form soft sticky dough. Stir in chives.

3 Drop dough by ¼ cupfuls 1½ inches apart onto prepared baking sheet.

4 Bake 15 to 16 minutes or until light golden brown. Remove to wire rack to cool slightly. Serve warm.

chile pecan biscuits

makes 9 to 10 biscuits

½ cup (1 stick) cold butter, divided

2 tablespoons jalapeño pepper,* minced (about 1 large)

⅓ cup finely chopped pecans

1 tablespoon honey

2 cups all-purpose flour

1 tablespoon baking powder

½ teaspoon salt

⅛ teaspoon chipotle chili powder

¼ teaspoon ground cumin

¾ cup milk

3½ tablespoons shredded sharp Cheddar cheese (optional)

Jalapeño peppers can sting and irritate the skin, so wear rubber gloves when handling, and do not touch your eyes.

1 Preheat oven to 425°F. Line baking sheet with parchment paper or spray with nonstick cooking spray.

2 Melt 1 tablespoon butter in small skillet over medium heat. Add jalapeño and pecans; cook and stir 3 to 5 minutes or until jalapeño is tender and pecans are fragrant. Stir in honey; remove from heat.

3 Combine flour, baking powder, salt, chili powder and cumin in large bowl; mix well. Cut remaining 7 tablespoons butter into small pieces. Cut butter into flour mixture with pastry blender or two knives until mixture resembles small crumbs. Stir in pecan mixture and milk; knead gently to form dough.

4 Turn out dough onto lightly floured surface; pat to ¾-inch thickness. Cut out biscuits with 2½-inch biscuit cutter, reworking dough as necessary. Place 1 inch apart on prepared baking sheet. Pat about 1½ teaspoons cheese onto each biscuit, if desired.

5 Bake 15 to 17 minutes or until golden brown. Remove to wire rack to cool slightly. Serve warm or at room temperature.

country buttermilk biscuits

makes about 9 biscuits

2 cups all-purpose flour

1 tablespoon baking powder

2 teaspoons sugar

½ teaspoon salt

½ teaspoon baking soda

⅓ cup cold shortening, cut into small pieces

⅔ cup buttermilk*

Or substitute 2½ teaspoons lemon juice plus enough milk to equal ⅔ cup. Stir; let stand 5 minutes before using.

1 Preheat oven to 450°F.

2 Combine flour, baking powder, sugar, salt and baking soda in medium bowl; mix well. Cut in shortening with pastry blender or two knives until mixture resembles coarse crumbs. Add buttermilk; stir until mixture forms soft dough that clings together and forms a ball.

3 Turn out dough onto well-floured surface. Knead dough gently 10 to 12 times; roll or pat to ½-inch thickness. Cut out biscuits with floured 2½-inch biscuit cutter. Place 2 inches apart on ungreased baking sheet.

4 Bake 8 to 10 minutes or until golden brown. Serve warm.

sour cream dill biscuits: Prepare Country Buttermilk Biscuits as directed in step 2, omitting buttermilk. Whisk ½ cup sour cream, ⅓ cup milk and 1 tablespoon chopped fresh dill *or* 1 teaspoon dried dill weed in small bowl until well blended. Add to flour mixture; continue as directed.

bacon and onion biscuits: Prepare Country Buttermilk Biscuits as directed in step 2, adding 4 slices crumbled crisp-cooked bacon and ⅓ cup chopped green onions to flour-shortening mixture before adding buttermilk. Continue as directed.

corn and sunflower seed biscuits

makes 12 biscuits

2 cups all-purpose flour

4 teaspoons baking powder

1 tablespoon sugar

½ teaspoon salt

½ teaspoon dried thyme

5 tablespoons cold butter, cut into thin slices

1 cup milk

1 cup corn*

⅓ cup plus 5 teaspoons salted roasted sunflower seeds, divided

Use fresh or thawed frozen corn; do not use supersweet corn.

1 Preheat oven to 400°F. Line baking sheet with parchment paper or spray with nonstick cooking spray.

2 Combine flour, baking powder, sugar, salt and thyme in large bowl; mix well. Cut in butter with pastry blender or two knives until mixture resembles coarse crumbs. Add milk; stir gently to form soft sticky dough. Stir in corn and ⅓ cup sunflower seeds.

3 Drop dough by ¼ cupfuls 1½ inches apart onto prepared baking sheet. Sprinkle ½ teaspoon sunflower seeds on each biscuit.

4 Bake 18 to 20 minutes or until biscuits are golden brown. Remove to wire rack to cool slightly. Serve warm.

cranberry scones

makes 8 scones

2 cups all-purpose flour

¼ cup sugar

2 teaspoons baking powder

½ teaspoon salt

¼ teaspoon baking soda

½ cup (1 stick) cold butter, cut into small pieces

⅔ cup buttermilk

1 egg

½ teaspoon vanilla

½ cup chopped pecans, toasted*

½ cup dried cranberries or cherries

*To toast pecans, spread on baking sheet; bake in preheated 350°F oven 8 to 10 minutes or until golden brown, stirring frequently.

1 Preheat oven to 350°F.

2 Combine flour, sugar, baking powder, salt and baking soda in large bowl; mix well. Cut in butter with pastry blender or two knives until mixture resembles coarse crumbs. Whisk buttermilk, egg and vanilla in small bowl until blended. Add to flour mixture; stir just until dry ingredients are moistened. Stir in pecans and cranberries.

3 Turn out dough onto floured surface. Shape into 6-inch circle; cut into eight wedges. Place 2 inches apart on ungreased baking sheet.

4 Bake 30 to 35 minutes or until golden brown. Serve warm.

coconut scones

makes 8 scones

1¾ cups all-purpose flour

½ teaspoon salt

1 tablespoon baking powder

2 tablespoons sugar

5 tablespoons cold butter,
   cut into small pieces

1 cup whipping cream, divided

½ cup plus ⅓ cup sweetened
   flaked coconut, divided

1 egg

2 tablespoons milk

2 teaspoons grated orange peel

Orange Butter
   (optional, recipe follows)

1 Preheat oven to 400°F. Line baking sheet with parchment paper.

2 Combine flour, salt, baking powder and sugar in large bowl; mix well. Cut in butter with pastry blender or two knives until mixture resembles coarse crumbs. Whisk ¾ cup cream, ½ cup coconut, egg, milk and orange peel in medium bowl until blended. Add flour mixture; stir just until dough forms.

3 Turn out dough onto lightly floured surface; pat into 8-inch circle about ¾ inch thick. Cut into eight wedges. Brush tops with remaining ¼ cup cream; sprinkle with remaining ⅓ cup coconut. Place 2 inches apart on prepared baking sheet.

4 Bake 12 to 15 minutes or until golden brown and coconut is toasted. Remove to wire rack to cool 15 minutes. Prepare Orange Butter, if desired. Serve with warm scones.

orange butter: Combine ½ cup (1 stick) softened butter, 2 tablespoons orange juice, 1 tablespoon grated orange peel and 2 teaspoons sugar in medium bowl; beat with electric mixer at low speed until creamy.

oat and whole wheat scones

makes 8 scones

1 cup old-fashioned oats

1 cup whole wheat flour

½ cup all-purpose flour

¼ cup sugar

1 tablespoon baking powder

¼ teaspoon salt

½ cup (1 stick) cold butter, cut into small pieces

½ cup whipping cream

1 egg

¾ cup dried cherries

1 Preheat oven to 425°F. Line baking sheet with parchment paper.

2 Combine oats, whole wheat flour, all-purpose flour, sugar, baking powder and salt in large bowl; mix well. Cut in butter with pastry blender or two knives until mixture resembles coarse crumbs. Whisk cream and egg in small bowl until blended. Add to flour mixture; stir just until dough comes together. Stir in cherries.

3 Turn out dough onto lightly floured surface; shape into 8-inch circle about ¾ inch thick. Cut into eight wedges; place 1 inch apart on prepared baking sheet.

4 Bake 18 to 20 minutes or until golden brown. Serve warm.

english-style scones

makes 6 scones

3 eggs, divided
½ cup whipping cream
1½ teaspoons vanilla
2 cups all-purpose flour
2 teaspoons baking powder
¼ teaspoon salt

¼ cup (½ stick) cold butter, cut into small pieces
¼ cup finely chopped pitted dates
¼ cup golden raisins or currants
1 teaspoon water

1 Preheat oven to 375°F. Line baking sheet with parchment paper.

2 Whisk 2 eggs, cream and vanilla in medium bowl until blended. Combine flour, baking powder and salt in medium bowl; mix well. Cut in butter with pastry blender or two knives until mixture resembles coarse crumbs. Stir in dates and raisins. Add cream mixture; stir just until dry ingredients are moistened.

3 Turn out dough onto lightly floured surface; knead four times with floured hands. Place dough on prepared baking sheet; pat into 8-inch circle. Gently score dough into six wedges with sharp wet knife, cutting three-fourths of the way through dough. Whisk remaining egg and water in small bowl; brush lightly over dough.

4 Bake 18 to 20 minutes or until golden brown. Remove to wire rack to cool 5 minutes. Cut into wedges; serve warm.

CAKES & CUPCAKES

apple ring coffeecake

3 cups all-purpose flour

1 teaspoon baking soda

1 teaspoon salt

1 teaspoon ground cinnamon

1 cup chopped walnuts

1½ cups granulated sugar

1 cup vegetable oil

2 eggs

2 teaspoons vanilla

2 medium tart apples,
    peeled and chopped

Powdered sugar

1. Preheat oven to 325°F. Spray 10-inch tube pan with nonstick cooking spray.

2. Sift flour, baking soda, salt and cinnamon into large bowl. Stir in walnuts.

3. Combine granulated sugar, oil, eggs and vanilla in medium bowl; mix well. Stir in apples. Add to flour mixture; stir just until blended. Spread batter evenly in prepared pan.

4. Bake 1 hour or until toothpick inserted near center comes out clean. Cool in pan 10 minutes. Loosen edges with metal spatula, if necessary. Remove to wire rack to cool completely. Sprinkle with powdered sugar just before serving.

chocolate yogurt snack cake

makes 12 to 15 servings

⅔ cup plus 2 tablespoons unsweetened Dutch process cocoa powder, divided

1¾ cups all-purpose flour

2 teaspoons baking powder

1 teaspoon salt

½ teaspoon baking soda

2 cups (16 ounces) whole-milk plain yogurt, divided

⅓ cup water

1 teaspoon vanilla

1¼ cups granulated sugar

6 tablespoons (¾ stick) butter, softened

2 eggs

1 cup semisweet chocolate chips

½ cup powdered sugar, sifted

1 Preheat oven to 350°F. Spray 13×9-inch baking pan with nonstick cooking spray. Dust with 2 tablespoons cocoa; tap out excess.

2 Combine remaining ⅔ cup cocoa, flour, baking powder, salt and baking soda in medium bowl; mix well. Whisk 1 cup yogurt, water and vanilla in small bowl until well blended.

3 Beat granulated sugar and butter in large bowl with electric mixer at medium speed 2 minutes or until light and fluffy. Add eggs; beat 1 minute. Gradually add flour mixture; beat at low speed just until combined. Add yogurt mixture; beat 1 minute, scraping down side of bowl once. Pour batter into prepared pan.

4 Bake 35 to 40 minutes or until toothpick inserted into center comes out clean. Cool completely in pan on wire rack.

5 Meanwhile, for frosting, combine chocolate chips and remaining 1 cup yogurt in medium microwavable bowl. Microwave on HIGH 30 seconds; stir. Continue microwaving at 10-second intervals until chocolate is melted and mixture is smooth. Whisk in powdered sugar until well blended. Spread over cooled cake.

cranberry pound cake

makes 10 to 12 servings

1½ cups sugar	4 eggs
1 cup (2 sticks) butter, softened	2 cups cake flour
¼ teaspoon salt	1 cup chopped fresh or thawed frozen cranberries
¼ teaspoon ground mace	

1 Preheat oven to 350°F. Grease and flour 9×5-inch loaf pan.

2 Beat sugar, butter, salt and mace in large bowl with electric mixer at medium speed 3 minutes or until light and fluffy. Add eggs, one at a time, beating well after each addition and scraping down side of bowl several times. Add flour, ½ cup at a time, beating at low speed after each addition until blended. Fold in cranberries. Spoon batter into prepared pan.

3 Bake 60 to 70 minutes or until toothpick inserted into center comes out clean. Cool in pan on wire rack 5 minutes. Run knife around edges of pan to loosen cake; cool 30 minutes. Remove to wire rack to cool completely.

note: You can make this cake when fresh or frozen cranberries aren't available. Cover 1 cup dried sweetened cranberries with hot water and let stand 10 minutes. Drain well before using. Add to batter in step 2 as directed.

carrot cake

makes 12 to 15 servings

2 cups all-purpose flour

2 teaspoons baking soda

2 teaspoons ground cinnamon, plus additional for garnish

1 teaspoon salt

2 cups sugar

1 cup vegetable oil

4 eggs

1 teaspoon vanilla

3 cups finely grated carrots (about 5 medium)

1 cup shredded coconut

1 can (8 ounces) crushed pineapple

1 cup chopped walnuts

Cream Cheese Frosting (page 140)

1 Preheat oven to 350°F. Spray 13×9-inch baking pan with nonstick cooking spray.

2 Combine flour, baking soda, 2 teaspoons cinnamon and salt in medium bowl; mix well. Beat sugar and oil in large bowl until well blended. Add eggs, one at a time, beating well after each addition. Beat in vanilla. Add flour mixture; stir until blended. Add carrots, coconut, pineapple and walnuts; stir just until blended. Pour batter into prepared pan.

3 Bake 45 to 50 minutes or until toothpick inserted into center comes out clean. Cool completely in pan on wire rack.

4 Prepare Cream Cheese Frosting; spread over cake. Sprinkle with additional cinnamon, if desired.

plum cake with streusel topping

makes 6 servings

Streusel Topping
(recipe follows)

1 cup plus 2 tablespoons
all-purpose flour

½ teaspoon baking powder

¼ teaspoon baking soda

¼ teaspoon salt

6 tablespoons (¾ stick) butter,
softened

¼ cup granulated sugar

¼ cup packed brown sugar

1 teaspoon vanilla

2 eggs

¼ cup buttermilk

3 medium plums, pitted and
each cut into 8 wedges*

*Plums should be underripe and
slightly soft to the touch.*

1 Preheat oven to 350°F. Spray 9-inch springform pan with nonstick cooking spray. Line bottom of pan with parchment paper; spray parchment paper with cooking spray.

2 Prepare Streusel Topping. Combine flour, baking powder, baking soda and salt in medium bowl; mix well.

3 Beat butter in large bowl with electric mixer at medium speed 1 minute. Add granulated sugar and brown sugar; beat 2 minutes or until light and fluffy. Beat in vanilla. Add eggs, one at a time, beating well after each addition. Alternately add flour mixture and buttermilk, beating at low speed after each addition. Spread batter in prepared pan.

4 Arrange plum wedges around outer edge of batter, reserving some for center. Sprinkle with Streusel Topping.

5 Bake 30 minutes or until cake springs back when lightly touched. Remove to wire rack. Remove side of pan; cool 20 minutes. Slide spatula under cake to transfer to serving plate. Serve warm or at room temperature.

streusel topping: Combine ¼ cup all-purpose flour, 3 tablespoons packed brown sugar and ½ teaspoon ground cinnamon in medium bowl; mix well. Add 2 tablespoons softened butter; mix with fingers until crumbly.

118

toffee crunch cheesecake

makes 10 to 12 servings

8 ounces chocolate cookies
or vanilla wafers, crushed

¼ cup (½ stick) butter, melted

3 packages (8 ounces each)
cream cheese, softened

½ cup granulated sugar

¼ cup packed brown sugar

3 eggs

1¾ cups (10-ounce package)
toffee baking bits, divided

1¼ teaspoons vanilla

Whipped cream (optional)

1 Preheat oven to 350°F. For crust, combine cookie crumbs and butter in small bowl; mix well. Press firmly into bottom of 9-inch springform pan.

2 For filling, beat cream cheese, granulated sugar and brown sugar in large bowl with electric mixer at medium speed 3 minutes or until smooth. Add eggs, one at a time, beating well after each addition. Reserve 1 tablespoon toffee bits; gently stir remaining toffee bits and vanilla into batter. Pour batter over crust.

3 Bake 45 to 50 minutes or until almost set. Remove to wire rack. Carefully run knife around edge of pan to loosen cheesecake. Cool completely; remove side of pan. Cover and refrigerate until cold.

4 Just before serving, top with whipped cream, if desired, and reserved toffee bits.

classic yellow cake

makes 12 servings

2¾ cups cake flour

1 tablespoon baking powder

¾ teaspoon salt

¾ cup (1½ sticks) butter, softened

1¾ cups sugar

3 eggs, at room temperature

2 egg yolks, at room temperature

¼ cup vegetable oil

2 teaspoons vanilla

1 cup whole milk, at room temperature

Vanilla Buttercream Frosting (page 141)

Colored sprinkles (optional)

1 Preheat oven to 350°F. Spray two 9-inch round cake pans with nonstick cooking spray; line bottoms with parchment paper.

2 Sift flour, baking powder and salt into medium bowl. Beat butter in large bowl with electric mixer at medium speed 2 minutes or until creamy. Add sugar; beat about 3 minutes or until light and fluffy. Add eggs and egg yolks, one at a time, beating well after each addition and scraping down side of bowl several times. Beat in oil and vanilla until blended.

3 Alternately add flour mixture and milk, beginning and ending with flour mixture; beat at low speed just until blended. Divide batter between prepared pans.

4 Bake 28 to 30 minutes or until toothpick inserted into centers comes out with few moist crumbs. Cool in pans 10 minutes; remove to wire racks to cool completely.

5 Prepare Vanilla Buttercream Frosting. Place one cake layer on serving plate; spread with 1 cup frosting. Top with remaining cake layer; frost top and side of cake. Top with sprinkles, if desired.

warm chocolate cakes

makes 4 servings

4 ounces bittersweet or
    semisweet chocolate

½ cup (1 stick) butter

2 eggs

2 egg yolks

¼ cup granulated sugar

¼ cup all-purpose flour

¼ teaspoon salt

    Powdered sugar (optional)

1 Preheat oven to 400°F. Spray four 6-ounce custard cups or soufflé dishes with nonstick cooking spray; place on baking sheet.

2 Melt chocolate and butter in small saucepan over very low heat or in microwave; cool slightly.

3 Meanwhile, beat eggs, egg yolks and granulated sugar in medium bowl with electric mixer at medium speed about 5 minutes or until thick and light in color. Add flour and salt; beat just until blended. Gently fold in chocolate mixture. Pour batter into prepared custard cups.

4 Bake about 9 minutes or until edges of cakes are set but centers are soft and move slightly when shaken. Let stand 2 minutes. Invert cakes onto individual serving plates; sprinkle with powdered sugar, if desired.

tip: The cakes can be made several hours in advance and baked just before serving. Prepare the batter as directed; cover and refrigerate until ready to bake. Bake at 400°F 10 to 11 minutes.

butterscotch malt zucchini cake

makes 10 to 12 servings

2½ cups all-purpose flour

4 tablespoons malted milk powder

1 teaspoon baking soda

½ teaspoon baking powder

½ teaspoon salt

½ teaspoon ground nutmeg

1¾ cups packed brown sugar

½ cup (1 stick) butter, softened

½ cup vegetable oil

2 eggs

½ cup buttermilk

1 teaspoon vanilla

2 cups grated zucchini

¾ cup white chocolate chips, divided

¾ cup butterscotch chips, divided

½ cup chopped nuts

1 Preheat oven to 350°F. Grease and flour 12-cup (10-inch) bundt pan.

2 Combine flour, malted milk powder, baking soda, baking powder, salt and nutmeg in medium bowl; mix well. Beat brown sugar, butter, oil and eggs in large bowl with electric mixer at medium speed 2 minutes. Add buttermilk and vanilla; beat until well blended.

3 Add flour mixture; beat at low speed just until blended. Stir in zucchini, ½ cup white chocolate chips, ½ cup butterscotch chips and chopped nuts. Pour batter into prepared pan.

4 Bake 60 to 65 minutes or until toothpick inserted near center comes out clean. Cool in pan 10 minutes; invert onto wire rack to cool completely.

5 Place remaining ¼ cup white chocolate chips in small microwavable bowl; microwave on HIGH 30 seconds. Stir; microwave at additional 10-second intervals until chocolate is melted and smooth, stirring frequently. Drizzle over cake. Repeat with remaining ¼ cup butterscotch chips. Drizzle melted chips over cake.

blueberry shortcakes

makes 12 shortcakes

shortcakes

- 2 cups all-purpose flour
- ½ cup packed brown sugar
- 4 teaspoons baking powder
- ¼ teaspoon ground nutmeg
- ½ cup (1 stick) cold butter, cut into small pieces
- ½ cup plus 1 tablespoon milk, divided
- 1 egg, at room temperature
- 1 teaspoon vanilla

filling

- 1 cup cold whipping cream
- 2 tablespoons powdered sugar
- ½ teaspoon vanilla
- 2 pints fresh blueberries

1 Position rack in center of oven. Preheat oven to 400°F. Line baking sheet with parchment paper.

2 Combine flour, brown sugar, baking powder and nutmeg in food processor; pulse to blend. Add butter; pulse 30 seconds or until mixture is crumbly and butter is in pea-sized pieces.

3 Whisk ½ cup milk, egg and 1 teaspoon vanilla in 2-cup measure until well blended. With motor running, pour mixture through feed tube; process about 30 seconds or until moist dough forms.

4 Turn out dough onto large piece of waxed paper dusted with flour; press into circle about ½ inch thick with floured hands. Cut out dough with 2¼-inch biscuit cutter; place 2 inches apart on prepared baking sheet. Gather scraps; knead lightly. Repeat process to make total of 12 rounds. Brush dough with remaining 1 tablespoon milk.

5 Bake 12 to 15 minutes or until golden brown. Remove to wire rack to cool completely.

6 Beat cream in medium bowl with electric mixer at medium speed 2 minutes or until it begins to thicken. Add powdered sugar and ½ teaspoon vanilla; beat 2 to 3 minutes or until soft peaks form. Split shortcakes; fill with whipped cream and blueberries. Serve immediately.

pumpkin streusel coffeecake

makes 9 to 12 servings

streusel

- ½ cup all-purpose flour
- ½ cup packed brown sugar
- 2 teaspoons ground cinnamon
- ¼ cup (½ stick) butter, softened
- ½ cup chopped walnuts

coffeecake

- 2 cups all-purpose flour
- 2 teaspoons baking powder
- ¾ teaspoon pumpkin pie spice
- ½ teaspoon baking soda
- ½ teaspoon salt
- ¾ cup packed brown sugar
- ½ cup (1 stick) butter, softened
- 2 eggs
- 1 cup canned pumpkin
- 2 teaspoons vanilla

1 Preheat oven to 325°F. Spray 8-inch square baking pan with nonstick cooking spray.

2 For streusel, combine ½ cup flour, ½ cup brown sugar and cinnamon in small bowl; mix well. Cut in ¼ cup butter with pastry blender or mix with fingertips until coarse crumbs form. Stir in walnuts. Refrigerate until ready to use.

3 For coffeecake, combine 2 cups flour, baking powder, pumpkin pie spice, baking soda and salt in medium bowl; mix well. Beat ¾ cup brown sugar and ½ cup butter in large bowl with electric mixer at medium-high speed 3 minutes or until light and fluffy. Add eggs, one at a time, beating well at medium speed after each addition. Beat in pumpkin and vanilla until well blended. Add flour mixture; beat at low speed until blended. (Batter will be very thick.) Spread half of batter in prepared baking pan; sprinkle with half of streusel. Top with remaining batter and streusel.

4 Bake about 40 minutes or until toothpick inserted into center comes out clean. Cool completely in pan on wire rack.

chocolate layer cake

makes 12 servings

2 cups all-purpose flour

1¾ cups sugar

⅔ cup unsweetened cocoa powder

2 teaspoons baking soda

1½ teaspoons baking powder

¾ teaspoon salt

1¾ cups buttermilk

½ cup vegetable oil

2 eggs

1 teaspoon vanilla

Creamy Chocolate Frosting
(page 140)

1 Preheat oven to 350°F. Line two 9-inch cake pans with parchment paper; spray pans and parchment paper with nonstick cooking spray.

2 Combine flour, sugar, cocoa, baking soda, baking powder and salt in large bowl; mix well. Whisk buttermilk, oil, eggs and vanilla in medium bowl until well blended. Add to flour mixture; stir until well blended. Divide batter evenly between prepared pans.

3 Bake 22 to 24 minutes or until toothpick inserted into centers comes out clean. Cool in pans 10 minutes; remove to wire racks to cool completely.

4 Prepare Creamy Chocolate Frosting. Place one cake layer on serving plate; spread with 1 cup frosting. Top with second cake layer; frost top and side of cake with remaining frosting. Refrigerate at least 1 hour before slicing.

glazed lemon loaf cake

makes 8 to 10 servings

cake

- 1½ cups all-purpose flour
- ½ teaspoon baking powder
- ½ teaspoon baking soda
- ½ teaspoon salt
- 1 cup granulated sugar
- 3 eggs
- ½ cup vegetable oil
- ⅓ cup lemon juice
- 2 tablespoons butter, melted
- 1 teaspoon lemon extract
- ½ teaspoon vanilla

glaze

- 3 tablespoons butter
- 1½ cups powdered sugar
- 2 tablespoons lemon juice
- 1 to 2 teaspoons grated lemon peel (optional)

1 Preheat oven to 350°F. Grease and flour 8×4-inch loaf pan.

2 For cake, combine flour, baking powder, baking soda and salt in large bowl; mix well. Whisk granulated sugar, eggs, oil, ⅓ cup lemon juice, 2 tablespoons melted butter, lemon extract and vanilla in medium bowl until well blended. Add to flour mixture; stir just until blended. Pour batter into prepared pan.

3 Bake about 40 minutes or until toothpick inserted into center comes out clean. Cool in pan 10 minutes; remove to wire rack to cool 10 minutes.

4 Meanwhile, prepare glaze. Melt 3 tablespoons butter in small saucepan over medium-low heat. Whisk in powdered sugar and 2 tablespoons lemon juice; cook until smooth and hot, whisking constantly. Pour glaze over warm cake; smooth top. Sprinkle with lemon peel, if desired. Cool completely before slicing.

black bottom cupcakes

makes 20 cupcakes

1 package (8 ounces) cream
cheese, softened

4 eggs, divided

⅓ cup plus ½ cup granulated sugar,
divided

2 cups all-purpose flour

1 cup packed brown sugar

¾ cup unsweetened cocoa powder

1 teaspoon baking powder

½ teaspoon baking soda

½ teaspoon salt

1 cup buttermilk

½ cup vegetable oil

1½ teaspoons vanilla

1 Preheat oven to 350°F. Line 20 standard (2½-inch) muffin cups with paper or foil
baking cups.

2 Beat cream cheese, 1 egg and ⅓ cup granulated sugar in small bowl until smooth.

3 Combine flour, brown sugar, cocoa, remaining ½ cup granulated sugar, baking
powder, baking soda and salt in large bowl; mix well. Whisk buttermilk, remaining
3 eggs, oil and vanilla in medium bowl until blended. Add to flour mixture; beat
2 minutes or until well blended.

4 Spoon batter evenly into prepared muffin cups. Spoon heaping tablespoon of cream
cheese mixture over batter in each cup; gently swirl with tip of knife to marbleize.

5 Bake 20 to 25 minutes or until toothpick inserted into centers comes out clean. Cool
in pans 10 minutes; remove to wire racks to cool completely.

peanut butter cupcakes

makes 24 cupcakes

2 cups all-purpose flour

2 teaspoons baking powder

½ teaspoon baking soda

½ teaspoon salt

1 cup creamy peanut butter, divided

¼ cup (½ stick) butter, softened

1 cup packed brown sugar

2 eggs

1 cup milk

1½ cups mini semisweet chocolate chips, divided, plus additional for garnish

Peanut Butter Frosting (page 141)

1 Preheat oven to 350°F. Line 24 standard (2½-inch) muffin cups with paper baking cups.

2 Combine flour, baking powder, baking soda and salt in small bowl; mix well. Beat ½ cup peanut butter and butter in large bowl with electric mixer at medium speed 2 minutes or until blended. Add brown sugar; beat until well blended. Add eggs, one at a time, beating well after each addition. Add flour mixture alternately with milk, beating at low speed until well blended. Stir in 1 cup chocolate chips. Spoon batter evenly into prepared muffin cups.

3 Bake 15 minutes or until toothpick inserted into centers comes out clean. (Cover loosely with foil if tops of cupcakes begin to brown too fast.) Cool completely in pans on wire racks.

4 Meanwhile, prepare Peanut Butter Frosting. Pipe or spread frosting over cupcakes.

5 Place remaining ½ cup peanut butter in small microwavable bowl; microwave on HIGH 15 seconds or until melted. Place remaining ½ cup chocolate chips in another small microwavable bowl; microwave on HIGH 15 seconds or until melted. Drizzle melted peanut butter and chocolate over frosting; garnish with additional chocolate chips.

cream cheese frosting

makes about 2 cups

1 package (8 ounces)
   cream cheese,
   softened
½ cup (1 stick) butter,
   softened
   Pinch salt
1½ cups powdered sugar
1 to 2 tablespoons milk
1 teaspoon vanilla

1 Beat cream cheese, butter and salt in large bowl with electric mixer at medium speed about 3 minutes or until light and creamy.

2 Add powdered sugar, 1 tablespoon milk and vanilla; beat at low speed until blended. Beat at medium speed 2 minutes or until frosting is smooth. Add additional milk for softer frosting, if desired.

note: This recipe makes enough frosting to frost a 13×9-inch cake. To frost a two-layer 9-inch cake or 18 to 24 cupcakes, double the recipe.

creamy chocolate frosting

makes about 3 cups

6 ounces unsweetened
   chocolate, chopped
½ cup (1 stick) butter,
   cubed
1½ cups sugar
1 cup whipping cream
1 teaspoon vanilla

1 Combine chocolate and butter in medium bowl. Heat sugar and cream in small saucepan over medium-high heat, stirring until sugar is dissolved. When cream begins to bubble, reduce heat to low and simmer 5 minutes.

2 Pour over chocolate mixture; stir until smooth. Stir in vanilla. Refrigerate until frosting is cool and thickened, stirring occasionally.

vanilla buttercream frosting

makes about 3 cups

1 cup (2 sticks) butter, softened

4 cups powdered sugar, sifted

2 teaspoons vanilla

Pinch salt

2 to 3 tablespoons milk

1 Beat butter in large bowl with electric mixer at medium speed 2 to 3 minutes or until smooth, creamy and lightened in color. Add powdered sugar, ½ cup at a time, beating at medium-high speed until well blended after each addition and scraping down side of bowl several times.

2 Add vanilla and salt; beat until blended. Add 2 tablespoons milk; beat at medium-high speed 3 minutes or until light and fluffy. If frosting is too thick, add additional milk, 1 teaspoon at a time; beat until well blended.

tip: For a brighter white frosting, use clear vanilla extract (available in many supermarkets and specialty stores). The dark color of standard vanilla extract will make the frosting an off-white color.

peanut butter frosting

makes about 3 cups

½ cup (1 stick) butter, softened

½ cup creamy peanut butter

2 cups sifted powdered sugar

½ teaspoon vanilla

Pinch salt

3 to 6 tablespoons milk

1 Beat butter and peanut butter in large bowl with electric mixer at medium speed about 2 minutes or until smooth. Gradually add powdered sugar, vanilla and salt; beat until well blended.

2 Add milk, 1 tablespoon at a time; beat until smooth and frosting reaches desired consistency.

141

PIES & TARTS

spiced pumpkin pie

makes 8 servings

Single-Crust Pie Dough
  (page 147) *or* 1 refrigerated
  pie crust (half of 15-ounce
  package)
1 can (16 ounces) pure pumpkin
¾ cup packed brown sugar
2 teaspoons ground cinnamon
¾ teaspoon ground ginger
½ teaspoon ground nutmeg,
  plus additional for garnish

¼ teaspoon salt
⅛ teaspoon ground cloves
4 eggs, lightly beaten
1 cup light cream or half-and-half
1 teaspoon vanilla
  Whipped cream (optional)

1 Prepare Single-Crust Pie Dough.

2 Preheat oven to 400°F. Roll out dough into 12-inch circle on lightly floured surface.
Line 9-inch pie plate with dough; trim and flute edge.

3 Whisk pumpkin and brown sugar in large bowl until blended. Stir in cinnamon,
ginger, ½ teaspoon nutmeg, salt and cloves. Add eggs; whisk until blended.
Gradually whisk in cream and vanilla until well blended. Pour into unbaked crust.

4 Bake 40 to 45 minutes or until knife inserted near center comes out clean. Cool
completely on wire rack. Serve warm or at room temperature; garnish with
whipped cream and additional nutmeg.

classic apple pie

makes 8 servings

1 package (15 ounces)
   refrigerated pie crusts
   (2 crusts)

6 cups sliced Granny Smith,
   Crispin or other firm-fleshed
   apples (about 6 medium)

½ cup sugar

1 tablespoon cornstarch

2 teaspoons lemon juice

½ teaspoon ground cinnamon

½ teaspoon vanilla

⅛ teaspoon salt

⅛ teaspoon ground nutmeg

⅛ teaspoon ground cloves

1 tablespoon whipping cream

1 Let one crust stand at room temperature 10 minutes. Preheat oven to 350°F. Line 9-inch pie plate with crust.

2 Combine apples, sugar, cornstarch, lemon juice, cinnamon, vanilla, salt, nutmeg and cloves in large bowl; toss to coat. Pour into crust. Place second crust over apples; press and crimp edge to seal. Cut four slits in top crust; brush with cream.

3 Bake 40 minutes or until crust is golden brown. Cool completely on wire rack.

peach raspberry pie

makes 8 servings

Single-Crust Pie Dough
(page 147)

Almond Crumb Topping
(recipe follows)

5 cups sliced peeled peaches
(about 2 pounds)

2 tablespoons lemon juice

1 cup fresh raspberries

½ cup sugar

2 tablespoons quick-cooking
tapioca

½ teaspoon ground cinnamon

¼ teaspoon ground nutmeg

1 Prepare Single-Crust Pie Dough and Almond Crumb Topping.

2 Preheat oven to 400°F. Roll out dough into 12-inch circle on floured surface. Line 9-inch pie plate with dough; flute edge. Refrigerate 15 minutes.

3 Place peaches in large bowl. Sprinkle with lemon juice; toss to coat. Gently stir in raspberries.

4 Combine sugar, tapioca, cinnamon and nutmeg in small bowl. Sprinkle over fruit mixture; toss gently to coat. Spoon into crust; sprinkle with topping.

5 Bake 15 minutes. *Reduce oven temperature to 350°F.* Bake 30 minutes or until crust is golden brown and filling is bubbly. Cool completely on wire rack.

almond crumb topping: Combine ⅔ cup old-fashioned or quick oats, ¼ cup all-purpose flour, ¼ cup packed brown sugar, ¼ cup slivered almonds and ½ teaspoon ground cinnamon in medium bowl; mix well. Stir in 3 tablespoons softened butter until mixture resembles coarse crumbs.

tip: To substitute frozen fruit, thaw 5 cups frozen peach slices in a large bowl for 1½ to 2 hours. Continue with step 3, using frozen raspberries (do not thaw). Bake as directed.

single-crust pie dough

makes dough for single-crust 9-inch pie

1¼ cups all-purpose flour

½ teaspoon salt

3 tablespoons cold shortening

3 tablespoons cold butter, cubed

3 to 4 tablespoons ice water

½ teaspoon cider vinegar

1 Combine flour and salt in medium bowl. Cut in shortening and butter with pastry blender or two knives until mixture resembles coarse crumbs.

2 Combine 3 tablespoons ice water and vinegar in small bowl. Add to flour mixture; mix with fork until dough forms, adding additional ice water as needed. Shape dough into a disc; wrap with plastic wrap. Refrigerate at least 30 minutes.

lemon-lime meringue pie

makes 8 servings

1 unbaked 9-inch deep-dish pie crust

4 eggs, separated

¾ cup plus 1 tablespoon sugar, divided

⅛ teaspoon salt

1 tablespoon cornstarch

½ cup whipping cream

3 tablespoons lemon juice

2 teaspoons grated lemon peel

3 tablespoons lime juice

2 teaspoons grated lime peel

2 tablespoons butter, cut into small pieces

1 Preheat oven to 400°F. Prick holes in bottom of crust with fork. Bake 10 minutes or until lightly browned. Cool completely on wire rack. *Reduce oven temperature to 325°F.*

2 Whisk egg yolks, ½ cup plus 1 tablespoon sugar and salt in medium saucepan until blended. Stir cornstarch into cream in small bowl until smooth. Whisk into egg yolk mixture. Add lemon juice, lemon peel, lime juice and lime peel; cook and stir over medium heat until thickened. Remove from heat; stir in butter until melted. Pour into crust.

3 Beat egg whites in medium bowl with electric mixer at medium speed until frothy. Add remaining ¼ cup sugar, 1 tablespoon at a time, beating at high speed after each addition until stiff and glossy. Gently spread meringue over filling, covering completely.

4 Bake 20 minutes or until meringue is golden brown. Cool completely on wire rack.

chocolate chess pie

makes 8 servings

4 ounces unsweetened chocolate, chopped

3 tablespoons butter

3 eggs

1 egg yolk

1¼ cups sugar

½ cup half-and-half

1 to 2 teaspoons instant coffee granules

¼ teaspoon salt

1 unbaked 9-inch pie crust

Whipped cream

Chocolate-covered coffee beans (optional)

1 Preheat oven to 325°F.

2 Combine chocolate and butter in small saucepan; heat over low heat until melted, stirring frequently. Set aside to cool 15 minutes.

3 Whisk eggs and egg yolk in medium bowl. Whisk in sugar, half-and-half, coffee granules and salt until well blended. Whisk in chocolate mixture until smooth. Pour into unbaked crust.

4 Bake 35 minutes or until set. Cool completely on wire rack. Refrigerate 2 hours or until ready to serve. Top with whipped cream; garnish with coffee beans.

note: Use 2 teaspoons instant coffee granules for a more pronounced coffee flavor; use a smaller amount if a more subtle coffee flavor is preferred.

apple crunch pie

makes 8 servings

1 refrigerated pie crust (half of 15-ounce package)

¾ cup all-purpose flour, divided

¼ cup packed brown sugar

¼ cup chopped walnuts

4 tablespoons (½ stick) butter, melted, divided

1¼ teaspoons ground cinnamon, divided

¾ teaspoon ground nutmeg, divided

1 cup granulated sugar

½ teaspoon ground ginger

¼ teaspoon salt

4 cups diced peeled apples

1 Preheat oven to 350°F. Line 9-inch pie plate with crust; flute edge as desired.

2 Combine ½ cup flour, brown sugar, walnuts, 2 tablespoons butter, ¼ teaspoon cinnamon and ¼ teaspoon nutmeg in small bowl; mix well. Spread in single layer on baking sheet. Bake 20 minutes on lowest rack of oven.

3 Combine remaining ¼ cup flour, 2 tablespoons butter, 1 teaspoon cinnamon, ½ teaspoon nutmeg, granulated sugar, ginger and salt in large bowl; mix well. Add apples; toss to coat. Pour apple mixture into prepared crust.

4 Bake 20 minutes on top rack of oven. Remove baking sheet from oven; let stand 5 minutes or until topping is cool enough to handle. Crumble over apple mixture.

5 Bake 25 to 35 minutes or until crust is golden brown and apples are tender. Cool completely on wire rack.

deep-dish blueberry pie

makes 8 servings

Double-Crust Pie Dough
(page 155)

6 cups fresh blueberries *or*
2 packages (16 ounces each)
frozen blueberries, thawed
and drained

2 tablespoons lemon juice

1¼ cups sugar

3 tablespoons quick-cooking
tapioca

¼ teaspoon ground cinnamon

1 tablespoon butter, cut into
small pieces

1 Prepare Double-Crust Pie Dough.

2 Preheat oven to 400°F. Place blueberries in large bowl; sprinkle with lemon juice. Combine sugar, tapioca and cinnamon in small bowl; mix well. Add to blueberries; stir gently until blended.

3 Roll out one disc of dough into 12-inch circle on lightly floured surface. Line 9-inch deep-dish pie plate with dough; trim all but ½ inch of overhang. Pour blueberry mixture into crust; dot with butter.

4 Roll out remaining disc of dough into 10-inch circle. Cut four or five shapes from dough with small cookie cutter or knife. Arrange dough over blueberry mixture; trim edge, leaving 1-inch border. Fold excess dough under and even with edge of pie plate. Crimp edge with fork.

5 Bake 15 minutes. *Reduce oven temperature to 350°F.* Bake 40 minutes or until crust is golden brown. Cool completely on wire rack.

double-crust pie dough

makes dough for double-crust 9-inch pie

2½ cups all-purpose flour
1 teaspoon salt
1 teaspoon sugar

1 cup (2 sticks) cold butter, cubed
⅓ cup ice water

1 Combine flour, salt and sugar in large bowl; mix well. Cut in butter with pastry blender or two knives until mixture resembles coarse crumbs.

2 Drizzle ice water over flour mixture, 2 tablespoons at a time, stirring just until dough comes together. Divide dough in half. Shape each half into a disc; wrap with plastic wrap. Refrigerate at least 30 minutes.

tip: Dough may be refrigerated up to 2 days or frozen up to 1 month. If frozen, thaw in refrigerator before using.

bourbon pecan pie

makes 8 servings

Single-Crust Pie Dough
(page 147)

¼ cup (½ stick) butter, softened

½ cup sugar

3 eggs

1½ cups light or dark corn syrup

2 tablespoons bourbon

1 teaspoon vanilla

1 cup pecan halves

1 Prepare Single-Crust Pie Dough.

2 Preheat oven to 350°F. Roll out dough into 12-inch circle on floured surface. Line 9-inch pie plate with dough; flute edge.

3 Beat butter in large bowl with electric mixer at medium speed 1 minute or until creamy. Add sugar; beat 3 minutes or until light and fluffy. Add eggs, one at a time, beating well after each addition. Add corn syrup, bourbon and vanilla; beat until well blended. Pour filling into crust. Arrange pecan halves on top.

4 Bake on lowest rack of oven 50 to 55 minutes or until knife inserted near center comes out clean. (Filling will be puffy.) Cool completely on wire rack. Serve at room temperature or cover and refrigerate up to 24 hours.

tip: For a shortcut version, use a 9-inch frozen pie crust (1½ inches deep) instead of making the crust from scratch. Prepare the filling and bake as directed.

lemon tart

makes 8 to 10 servings

1 refrigerated pie crust (half
  of 15-ounce package)
5 eggs
1 tablespoon cornstarch

1 cup sugar
½ cup (1 stick) butter
½ cup lemon juice

1 Position rack in center of oven. Preheat oven to 450°F.

2 Line 9-inch tart pan with crust, pressing to fit securely against side of pan. Trim off any excess crust. Prick bottom and side of crust with fork.

3 Bake 9 to 10 minutes or until golden brown. Cool completely on wire rack. *Reduce oven temperature to 350°F.*

4 Meanwhile, whisk eggs and cornstarch in medium bowl until blended. Combine sugar, butter and lemon juice in small saucepan; cook and stir over medium-low heat just until butter melts. Whisk in egg mixture; cook 8 to 10 minutes or until thickened, stirring constantly. (Do not let mixture come to a boil.) Pour into medium bowl; stir 1 minute or until cooled slightly. Let cool 10 minutes.

5 Pour cooled lemon curd into baked crust. Bake 25 to 30 minutes or until set. Cool completely on wire rack. Store leftovers in refrigerator.

ginger plum tart

makes 6 to 8 servings

1 refrigerated pie crust (half of 15-ounce package)

1¾ pounds plums, cut into ½-inch slices

½ cup plus 1 teaspoon sugar, divided

1½ tablespoons all-purpose flour

1½ teaspoons ground ginger

¼ teaspoon ground cinnamon

⅛ teaspoon salt

1 egg

2 teaspoons water

1 Preheat oven to 400°F. Let pie crust stand at room temperature 10 minutes.

2 Combine plums, ½ cup sugar, flour, ginger, cinnamon and salt in large bowl; toss to coat.

3 Roll out crust into 14-inch circle on lightly floured surface. Transfer crust to large (10-inch) ungreased cast iron skillet. Mound plum mixture in center of crust, leaving 2-inch border around fruit. Fold crust in over filling, overlapping and pleating as necessary and gently pressing crust into fruit to secure.

4 Beat egg and water in small bowl; brush over crust. Sprinkle with remaining 1 teaspoon sugar.

5 Bake about 45 minutes or until crust is golden brown. Cool completely on wire rack.

french silk tart

makes 12 servings

1½ cups finely chopped chocolate sandwich cookies (about 15 cookies)

⅓ cup butter, melted

1½ cups whipping cream

1¼ cups semisweet chocolate chips

1 tablespoon unsweetened Dutch process cocoa powder*

2 cups thawed frozen whipped topping

Grated chocolate (optional)

Natural unsweetened cocoa powder may be substituted. Dutch process cocoa powder has a stronger flavor and will be darker color after baking.

1 Combine cookie crumbs and butter in small bowl; mix well. Press firmly into bottom of 10-inch springform pan. Refrigerate until ready to fill.

2 Pour cream into medium microwavable bowl; microwave on HIGH 1 to 1½ minutes or just until hot and bubbles appear around edge. Add chocolate chips; stir until melted. Add cocoa; mix well. Refrigerate 1 hour or until cold and slightly thickened.

3 Beat chilled chocolate mixture with electric mixer at medium speed just until soft peaks form. *Do not overbeat.*

4 Spread chocolate mixture over crust; spread whipped topping over chocolate layer. Garnish with grated chocolate.

apple galettes

makes 5 galettes

1 tablespoon butter

4 medium Granny Smith, Crispin or other firm-fleshed apples, peeled and cut into ¾-inch pieces (about 4 cups)

6 tablespoons granulated sugar

½ teaspoon ground cinnamon

⅛ teaspoon salt

2 teaspoons cornstarch

2 teaspoons lemon juice

1 refrigerated pie crust (half of 15-ounce package)

1 egg, beaten

1 tablespoon sparkling or granulated sugar

1 Melt butter in medium saucepan over medium heat. Add apples, granulated sugar, cinnamon and salt; cook 10 minutes or until apples are tender, stirring occasionally. Drain apples in colander set over medium bowl; pour liquid back into saucepan. Cook over medium-high heat until liquid is slightly syrupy and reduced by half. Add cornstarch; cook and stir 1 minute.

2 Combine apples, lemon juice and cornstarch mixture in medium bowl; stir to coat. Set aside to cool to room temperature.

3 Preheat oven to 425°F. Line large baking sheet with parchment paper. Unroll pie crust on work surface; cut out five circles with 4-inch round cookie cutter. Place dough circles on prepared baking sheet.

4 Divide apples evenly among dough circles, piling apples in center of each circle and leaving ½-inch border. Fold dough in over filling, overlapping and pleating as necessary and gently pressing dough into fruit to secure. Brush dough lightly with beaten egg; sprinkle with coarse sugar.

5 Bake about 25 minutes or until crusts are golden brown. Cool on wire rack.

rustic plum tart

makes 8 servings

¼ cup (½ stick) plus 1 tablespoon butter, divided

3 cups sliced plums (about 6 medium, cut into 8 wedges each)

¼ cup granulated sugar

½ cup all-purpose flour

½ cup old-fashioned or quick oats

¼ cup packed brown sugar

½ teaspoon ground cinnamon

¼ teaspoon salt

1 egg

1 teaspoon water

1 refrigerated pie crust (half of 15-ounce package)

1 tablespoon chopped crystallized ginger

1 Preheat oven to 425°F. Line baking sheet with parchment paper.

2 Melt 1 tablespoon butter in large skillet over high heat. Add plums; cook and stir 3 minutes or until softened. Stir in granulated sugar; cook 1 minute or until juices are thickened. Remove from heat; set aside.

3 Combine flour, oats, brown sugar, cinnamon and salt in medium bowl; mix well. Cut remaining ¼ cup butter into small pieces. Cut butter into flour mixture with pastry blender or two knives until mixture resembles coarse crumbs.

4 Beat egg and water in small bowl. Unroll pie crust on prepared baking sheet; brush lightly with egg mixture. Sprinkle with ¼ cup oat mixture, leaving 1½-inch border around edge of crust. Spoon plums over oat mixture, leaving juices in skillet. Sprinkle with ginger. Fold crust in over filling, overlapping and pleating as necessary. Sprinkle with remaining oat mixture. Brush edge of crust with egg mixture.

5 Bake 25 minutes or until crust is golden brown. Cool on wire rack.

COBBLERS & CRISPS

strawberries and cream cobbler

makes 6 servings

2 pounds fresh strawberries, hulled and sliced

½ cup strawberry jam

⅔ cup all-purpose flour

⅓ cup sugar

1 teaspoon baking powder

¼ teaspoon salt

2 tablespoons cold butter, cut into small pieces

¼ cup milk

6 tablespoons whipping cream or melted vanilla ice cream

1 Preheat oven to 375°F. Spray six 8-ounce ramekins or custard cups with nonstick cooking spray.

2 Combine strawberries and jam in large skillet; cook over medium heat about 20 minutes or until thickened and reduced, stirring occasionally.

3 Meanwhile, combine flour, sugar, baking powder and salt in medium bowl; mix well. Cut in butter with pastry blender or two knives until mixture resembles fine crumbs. Stir in milk to make soft dough.

4 Divide strawberry mixture evenly among prepared ramekins. Spoon dough evenly over strawberry mixture, spreading with back of spoon.

5 Bake 20 to 25 minutes or until crust is golden brown. Serve warm; drizzle each cobbler with 1 tablespoon cream.

peach-cranberry cobbler
with corn bread biscuits

makes 6 servings

1 package (16 ounces) frozen
  sliced peaches, thawed

1 cup fresh or frozen cranberries
  or raspberries

⅓ cup orange juice

¼ cup packed brown sugar

⅓ cup plus 2 tablespoons
  all-purpose flour, divided

⅛ teaspoon ground allspice

3 tablespoons yellow cornmeal

1 tablespoon granulated sugar

1 teaspoon baking powder

¼ teaspoon salt

2 tablespoons cold butter,
  cut into small pieces

1 egg

3 tablespoons milk

1 Preheat oven to 400°F.

2 Combine peaches, cranberries and orange juice in large bowl; mix well. Combine brown sugar, 2 tablespoons flour and allspice in small bowl. Add to peach mixture; toss to coat. Spoon into 8-inch square baking dish.

3 Combine remaining ⅓ cup flour, cornmeal, granulated sugar, baking powder and salt in medium bowl; mix well. Cut in butter with pastry blender or two knives until mixture resembles coarse crumbs. Whisk egg and milk in small bowl; stir into flour mixture with fork just until moistened. Spoon topping evenly over fruit mixture.

4 Bake 30 to 35 minutes or until toothpick inserted into topping comes out clean.

variation: For individual cobblers, divide fruit and topping mixtures evenly among six 8-ounce custard cups or ramekins. Bake 20 to 25 minutes or until toothpick inserted into topping comes out clean.

COBBLERS & CRISPS

nectarine-raspberry cobbler

makes 4 to 6 servings

3 cups sliced peeled
   nectarines or peaches
   (about 1¼ pounds)

½ cup fresh raspberries

4 tablespoons sugar, divided

1 tablespoon cornstarch

½ teaspoon ground cinnamon

¾ cup all-purpose flour

1 teaspoon grated lemon peel

¾ teaspoon baking powder

¼ teaspoon salt

⅛ teaspoon baking soda

3 tablespoons cold butter,
   cut into small pieces

½ cup buttermilk

1 Preheat oven to 375°F.

2 Combine nectarines and raspberries in large bowl. Combine 3 tablespoons sugar, cornstarch and cinnamon in small bowl. Add to fruit; toss gently to coat. Spoon into 8-inch round baking dish.

3 Combine flour, lemon peel, baking powder, salt, baking soda and remaining 1 tablespoon sugar in medium bowl; mix well. Cut in butter with pastry blender or two knives until mixture resembles coarse crumbs. Stir in buttermilk until blended. Drop dough in six equal spoonfuls over fruit mixture.

4 Bake 25 to 27 minutes or until filling is bubbly and topping is beginning to brown. Serve warm.

note: One pound of frozen unsweetened peach slices and ½ cup frozen unsweetened raspberries may be substituted for the fresh fruit. Let the peach slices stand at room temperature at least 2 hours or until almost thawed and use the raspberries frozen. Bake an additional 3 to 5 minutes or until the filling is bubbly and the topping is beginning to brown.

pear and cranberry cobbler

makes 6 to 8 servings

filling

- 4 cups diced peeled ripe pears (3 to 4 medium)
- 2 cups fresh cranberries
- ½ cup sugar
- 3 tablespoons all-purpose flour
- ¼ teaspoon ground cinnamon
- 2 tablespoons butter, cut into small pieces

topping

- 1 cup all-purpose flour
- 2 tablespoons sugar
- 2 teaspoons baking powder
- ¼ teaspoon salt
- ¼ cup (½ stick) cold butter, cut into small pieces
- ½ cup milk

1 Preheat oven to 375°F. Spray 10-inch round or oval baking dish with nonstick cooking spray.

2 For filling, combine pears, cranberries, ½ cup sugar, 3 tablespoons flour and cinnamon in large bowl; toss to coat. Spoon into prepared baking dish; dot with 2 tablespoons butter.

3 For topping, combine 1 cup flour, 2 tablespoons sugar, baking powder and salt in medium bowl; mix well. Cut in ¼ cup cold butter with pastry blender or two knives until mixture resembles coarse crumbs. Stir in milk to make soft sticky dough. Drop dough by tablespoonfuls over fruit mixture. Place baking dish on baking sheet.

4 Bake 25 to 35 minutes or until filling is bubbly and topping is golden brown. Serve warm.

brown butter blueberry peach cobbler

makes 8 servings

3 tablespoons butter

4 packages (16 ounces each) frozen sliced peaches, thawed and drained

1 cup fresh blueberries

½ cup packed brown sugar

1¼ cups all-purpose flour, divided

½ teaspoon vanilla

¼ teaspoon ground nutmeg

2 tablespoons granulated sugar

1½ teaspoons baking powder

½ teaspoon salt

¼ cup milk

3 tablespoons butter, melted

1 Preheat oven to 375°F.

2 Melt 3 tablespoons butter in large skillet (not nonstick) over medium heat. Cook and stir 3 minutes or until butter has nutty aroma and turns light brown in color. Add peaches; cook and stir 2 minutes.

3 Combine peaches, blueberries, brown sugar, ¼ cup flour, vanilla and nutmeg in large bowl; toss gently to coat. Spoon into 2-quart baking dish.

4 Bake 10 minutes. Meanwhile, combine remaining 1 cup flour, granulated sugar, baking powder and salt in medium bowl; mix well. Stir in milk and 3 tablespoons melted butter until blended. Drop eight equal spoonfuls of batter over warm fruit mixture.

5 Bake 30 to 35 minutes or until biscuits are deep golden brown and cooked on bottom. Cool 10 minutes. Serve warm.

tip: The deep, nutty taste of brown butter adds extra flavor to this crisp. When browning butter, use a pan with a light-colored bottom so you can see the color changes as the butter cooks—it will turn from pale and opaque to yellow to caramel colored and then golden brown. Keep stirring as the butter melts and becomes foamy; you'll begin to see small brown bits (the milk solids) on the bottom of the pan that will toast and give off a very rich, buttery aroma. It's important to watch the butter closely as it turns color, because it can go from golden brown to burnt very quickly.

tangy cranberry cobbler

makes 6 servings

2 cups thawed frozen or fresh cranberries

1 cup dried cranberries

1 cup raisins

½ cup orange juice

¼ cup plus 2 tablespoons sugar, divided

2 teaspoons cornstarch

1 cup all-purpose flour

2 teaspoons baking powder

1 teaspoon ground cinnamon

¼ teaspoon salt

¼ cup (½ stick) cold butter, cut into small pieces

½ cup milk

1 Preheat oven to 400°F.

2 Combine cranberries, dried cranberries, raisins, orange juice, ¼ cup sugar and cornstarch in 9-inch square baking dish; toss to coat.

3 Combine flour, remaining 2 tablespoons sugar, baking powder, cinnamon and salt in large bowl; mix well. Cut in butter with pastry blender or two knives until mixture resembles coarse crumbs. Add milk; stir just until moistened. Drop batter by large spoonfuls over cranberry mixture.

4 Bake 35 to 40 minutes or until topping is light golden brown. Serve warm.

apple blackberry crisp

makes 6 servings

4 cups sliced peeled apples
  Juice of ½ lemon

2 tablespoons granulated sugar

1 teaspoon ground cinnamon, divided

1 cup old-fashioned oats

6 tablespoons (¾ stick) cold butter, cut into small pieces

⅔ cup packed brown sugar

¼ cup all-purpose flour

1 cup fresh blackberries

  Whipped cream (optional)

1 Preheat oven to 375°F. Spray 9-inch oval or 8-inch square baking dish with nonstick cooking spray.

2 Place apples in large bowl; drizzle with lemon juice. Add granulated sugar and ½ teaspoon cinnamon; toss to coat.

3 Combine oats, butter, brown sugar, flour and remaining ½ teaspoon cinnamon in food processor; pulse until combined, leaving some large pieces.

4 Gently stir blackberries into apple mixture. Spoon into prepared baking dish; sprinkle with oat mixture.

5 Bake 30 to 40 minutes or until filling is bubbly and topping is golden brown. Serve with whipped cream, if desired.

tip: This crisp can also be made without the blackberries; just add an additional 1 cup sliced apples.

triple berry crisp

makes 8 servings

2 cups frozen blackberries, thawed, undrained

2 cups frozen raspberries, thawed, undrained

1 cup frozen blueberries, thawed, undrained

½ cup plus 3 tablespoons all-purpose flour, divided

⅓ cup granulated sugar

1½ teaspoons grated fresh ginger

1 teaspoon vanilla

½ cup old-fashioned oats

¼ teaspoon ground cinnamon

¼ cup (½ stick) butter, cut into small pieces

¼ cup slivered almonds

3 tablespoons packed dark brown sugar

1 Preheat oven to 350°F. Spray 9-inch square baking dish with nonstick cooking spray.

2 Combine blackberries, raspberries, blueberries, 3 tablespoons flour, granulated sugar, ginger and vanilla in large bowl; toss gently to coat. Spoon into prepared baking dish.

3 Combine remaining ½ cup flour, oats and cinnamon in medium bowl; mix well. Cut in butter with pastry blender or two knives until mixture resembles coarse crumbs. Spoon evenly over berry mixture. Top with almonds; sprinkle with brown sugar.

4 Bake 30 minutes or until filling is bubbly and topping is golden brown. Cool on wire rack 30 minutes.

strawberry rhubarb crisp

makes 8 servings

4 cups sliced rhubarb
(1-inch pieces)

3 cups sliced fresh strawberries
(about 1 pint)

¾ cup granulated sugar

⅓ cup plus ¼ cup all-purpose flour,
divided

1 tablespoon grated lemon peel

1 cup quick oats

½ cup packed brown sugar

1 teaspoon ground cinnamon

½ teaspoon salt

⅓ cup butter, melted

1 Preheat oven to 375°F. Combine rhubarb and strawberries in large bowl.

2 Combine granulated sugar, ¼ cup flour and lemon peel in small bowl. Sprinkle over fruit; toss to coat. Spoon into 9-inch square baking dish.

3 Combine oats, brown sugar, remaining ⅓ cup flour, cinnamon and salt in medium bowl; mix well. Stir in butter until crumbly. Sprinkle over fruit mixture.

4 Bake 45 to 50 minutes or until filling is bubbly and topping is lightly browned. Serve warm or at room temperature.

cranberry apple crisp

makes 6 to 8 servings

1 cup packed brown sugar, divided

1 tablespoon cornstarch

1 teaspoon ground cinnamon

½ teaspoon ground ginger

¼ teaspoon ground nutmeg

5 to 6 cups cubed peeled tart apples

1 cup fresh or frozen cranberries *or* ½ cup dried cranberries

1 teaspoon grated orange peel

½ cup all-purpose flour

½ cup old-fashioned oats

½ cup coarsley chopped walnuts

½ teaspoon salt

¼ cup (½ stick) cold butter, cut into small pieces

1 Preheat oven to 350°F. Spray shallow 2-quart baking dish with nonstick cooking spray.

2 Combine ½ cup brown sugar, cornstarch, cinnamon, ginger and nutmeg in large bowl. Add apples, cranberries and orange peel; toss to coat. Spoon into prepared baking dish.

3 Combine flour, oats, walnuts, remaining ½ cup brown sugar and salt in medium bowl; mix well. Cut in butter with pastry blender or two knives until mixture resembles coarse crumbs. Sprinkle over fruit mixture.

4 Bake 50 minutes or until apples are tender. Serve warm.

INDEX

INDEX

INDEX

metric conversion chart

VOLUME MEASUREMENTS (dry)

1/8 teaspoon = 0.5 mL
1/4 teaspoon = 1 mL
1/2 teaspoon = 2 mL
3/4 teaspoon = 4 mL
1 teaspoon = 5 mL
1 tablespoon = 15 mL
2 tablespoons = 30 mL
1/4 cup = 60 mL
1/3 cup = 75 mL
1/2 cup = 125 mL
2/3 cup = 150 mL
3/4 cup = 175 mL
1 cup = 250 mL
2 cups = 1 pint = 500 mL
3 cups = 750 mL
4 cups = 1 quart = 1 L

VOLUME MEASUREMENTS (fluid)

1 fluid ounce (2 tablespoons) = 30 mL
4 fluid ounces (1/2 cup) = 125 mL
8 fluid ounces (1 cup) = 250 mL
12 fluid ounces (1 1/2 cups) = 375 mL
16 fluid ounces (2 cups) = 500 mL

WEIGHTS (mass)

1/2 ounce = 15 g
1 ounce = 30 g
3 ounces = 90 g
4 ounces = 120 g
8 ounces = 225 g
10 ounces = 285 g
12 ounces = 360 g
16 ounces = 1 pound = 450 g

DIMENSIONS

1/16 inch = 2 mm
1/8 inch = 3 mm
1/4 inch = 6 mm
1/2 inch = 1.5 cm
3/4 inch = 2 cm
1 inch = 2.5 cm

OVEN TEMPERATURES

250°F = 120°C
275°F = 140°C
300°F = 150°C
325°F = 160°C
350°F = 180°C
375°F = 190°C
400°F = 200°C
425°F = 220°C
450°F = 230°C

BAKING PAN SIZES

Utensil	Size in Inches/Quarts	Metric Volume	Size in Centimeters
Baking or Cake Pan (square or rectangular)	8×8×2	2 L	20×20×5
	9×9×2	2.5 L	23×23×5
	12×8×2	3 L	30×20×5
	13×9×2	3.5 L	33×23×5
Loaf Pan	8×4×3	1.5 L	20×10×7
	9×5×3	2 L	23×13×7
Round Layer Cake Pan	8×1½	1.2 L	20×4
	9×1½	1.5 L	23×4
Pie Plate	8×1¼	750 mL	20×3
	9×1¼	1 L	23×3
Baking Dish or Casserole	1 quart	1 L	—
	1½ quart	1.5 L	—
	2 quart	2 L	—